SELF-TUTOR FOR JAZZ PIANO (BAND & SOLO)

by Cedric Thompson

Copyright © 2021 Cedric Thompson

The right of the author to be identified as the author of this work has been asserted in accordance with the Copyright, Designs and Patents Act 1988.

All rights reserved.

No part of this publication may be reproduced, stored in a retrieval system, or transmitted, in any form or by any means, electronic, mechanical, photocopying, recording or otherwise, without the prior permission of the copyright owners.

ISBN: 978-1-910779-84-2

Sheet music used in this book has been interpreted by the author and is used for illustration purposes only. Copyright of the songs remains that of the original owner.

Preface

The Author has spent most of his career in Universities; he has four degrees, two of them higher, from London, Leeds and Sheffield. Applying his experience of teaching Maths, Physics and Electronics to explaining musical concepts to readers, listeners and players has been a great pleasure. He has played the vibes and the piano in various jazz bands around the country, tried to make the subject interesting through questions and answers in the book, and given lessons to players. The book is written in a simple language and you should not need a tutor.

For readers who want to learn to play piano solo or band need not pay attention to Chapter 7. Scales (you need them); chords (most important) including playing the II, V, I cadence, and the real experience of accompanying or soloing with the CD music. This CD is easy to buy from Amazon or a good local shop (see reference section at the back of this book). You are then equipped to go on to 'play alongs' – Reference 2.

Contents

Preface	3
Chapter 1 - Introduction	6
Chapter 2 - Scales	8
2.1 Major scale in C	8
2.2 Minor Scales.	11
2.3. Dominant 7th SCALES	12
Chapter 3 - Chords	13
3.1 Major chords for solo	13
3.2 Minor chords for solo	13
3.3 C7= CEGB*b* Dominant seventh.	14
3.4 Other chords (SOLO)	14
3.5 Chords for band pianists.	15
Chapter 4 - Circle of Fifths	18
4.1 Practice with two handed chords.	22
4.2 "Round the Clock on the 251"	24
4.3 Exercise going 'round the clock' using both hands for the chord playing.	24
Chapter 5 - Playing along	29
5.1 Playing the four pieces of music using your CD.	29
Chapter 6 - Inprovisation	33
6.1 Minor Chord Improvisation	33
6.2 Walking Tenths	35
6.3 Pentatonic chords/scale	37
Chapter 7 - History of the Piano Keyboard	39
Chapter 8 - Four sheets of music	45
8.1 Moment's Notice	45
8.3 I'm Old Fashioned Solos	47
8.4 Lazy Bird	48
8.5 Blue Trane, John Coltrane	50
Chapter 9 - Answers	51
Glossary	54
References	67
Acknowledgements	68
Dedication	68
Contacting the Author	68

Introduction – How people end up playing Jazz

The author started playing Jazz as a vibes player, but went on to play the piano after attending a year's course in Jazz every Saturday. Unless you become a professional you won't earn much money from playing in pubs. You have to like what you hear, from wherever, to make you want to contribute. Some youngsters play the clarinet at school, maybe even in a school band; this instrument is a natural starter pupils can learn from grades in music, be they flute, violin, piano. With regard to piano, the music sheets have bass and treble clef, Oscar Petersen was trained classically, and he went on to become a top Jazz Pianist. Music is presents in this book with treble clef and bass chords. In some jazz bands the conductor issues out music sheets in concert, Bflat, Eflat and bass, for immediate playing. The concert C is often displayed with chords only, on many occasions. i.e no melody line (which is the treble). If the Pianist is requested to play a solo from chords only (accompanies by bass player and drums), the only type of playing from the music is by improvisation. This type of performing is not random note generation, it is playing the music based on the chords in the music sheet. This can only be achieved by knowing the music scales, and being able to reproduce excerpts from these to fill 32 bars of music – on time!

Some people can actually count the 1234 beats/bar through a tune without thinking about it, solos by other instrumentalists are no easier. They have the tune before them, they are taught to read along the lines of treble clef (which is the melody) as the song proceeds. There is much less improvisation in classical concerts, but if you've watched a performance on TV, you can't help but noticing that in the case of bowed instruments (all stringed instruments are bowed, unless plucked of course), the bows of, say, the violins all move in sync; i.e. back and forth at the same time.

These artists (all professional) and absolutely all in time with on another; they keep this up through the whole symphony. The same applies to jazz-band performers, timing their played notes in sync.

You can, as you read this introduction, realise that a number of topics are included in this book:- timing, chords, scales improvisation. Each topic warrants a chapter. There is more to involve yourself with – keenness, enthusiasm, these two attributes drive you to produce the sounds of jazz. As you progress through the book, some of which you would already know, there are, in my opinion certain highlights, of achievement; I'll give you two of these:

(i) the first is what we call 251, expressed II, V, I. In three specially selected chords, a tension is introduced on the II-7^1, and it resolves partially on the V7, and final resolution is achieved o the I Δ^2. It is rather like two people first arguing,

---

1   Minor chord is – Dominant seventh = V7
2   Δ = Major

then partially agreeing and finally fully agreeing. The cinema does this, spread over 90 mins – love finds a way; the audience walks away happy.

You will not realise until you read the music, hear the notes that such a thing (i.e. the 251) has happened, albeit very quickly.

(ii) a great personal satisfaction (and even an ovation if there's and audience) from a piano improvising accompanied by double bass; it takes a lot of practice, and the pianist must know there scales, at sight and "fit it all" in the time allotted. It could also include notes from the melody, if they're given. There are questions, usually at the end of each chapter; the answers are all given in a section near the end of each chapter; the answers are all given near the rear end of the book. In orders to cut the cost of this book, a CD is not provided but one can be purchased for £5.00 from Amazon. (John Coltrane, blue note 53428, more information in the reference section).

This CD has tunes for which the music has been written In the book (Chapter 8). The notes in these four sheets have been written by your author to match the sounds produces by the instrumentalists, also in chords in the music sheets, there are selected from various sources available including the author's own versions. Of the seven tunes in the CD, "*Moments Notice*", "*Lazy Bird*", "*I'm Old Fashioned*" and "*Blue Trane*" give you the chance to play along with either chords only, or treble notes only – these are the four titles of the music provided in this book. The music is hand-written. Hopefully this book should provide you with sufficient training to play solo or in a band. For training – further, with a good and well organised playalong music book with a CD. See a reference 2 at the back of the book.

In order to know more about the piano you play and its development through history with efforts by historical musical experts of their time, read this chapter. Pythagorous, Schoenberg, and Galilei[3], finally giving rise to the concept of (*see Ref.3) equal temperament. – chapter 7, see glossary, under 'T'. The piano is a remarkable instrument and deserves your best efforts to master it in the way you find best, be it solo or in a band.

The glossary has been used not only for musical terms but also elementary mathematical concepts, and musical technology. Chapter 5 contains these concepts which are used to show difficulties in approving Pythagorous's concepts; or disapproving! Understanding this work does little to improve a pianist's playing ability, it just gives the student incentive to improve and work hard. You will carry this ability with you for life, and enjoy playing along after you've retired

---

3   Historical musical experts

Chapter 2 - Scales

A scale is progression of notes in ascending or descending order. A note is a single sound of definite pitch and duration, which can be identified in writing. All notes have a definite pitch and duration, which can be identified in writing. All notes have a definite pitch and duration assigned to them. The absolute pitch is 440 vibrations per second, abbreviated cycles/sec (c/s) or hertz (Hz), it is shown on the piano as a letter `A` above middle C. (Fig 2.1). This key, so worded as middle because it is located at about the middle of a Piano, and is shaded in FIG 2.1. A chromatic scale covers both the white notes and black notes; the latter are referred to sharps and flats. A sharp raises the pitch of a natural note, by a semitone making it C sharp[4]. A flat lowers the pitch of a natural note, by a semitone, symbolised as C*b* and called C flat (symbol *b*).

Note the B*b* = A# F# = G*b* C## = D.

> Q. 2.1 Write down the note represented by
>
> (i) G##
>
> (ii) C# *b*

Keyboards vary in size from three to seven octaves, (an octave is defined as doubling of the frequence, or tone) In the diagram of fig 2.1 the key shaded is middle C. Six full octaves. All future keyboard diagrams will have one shaded key, representing middle C.Fig 2.1

Fig 2.1

2.1 Major scale in C

The symbol for Major is Δ.

Playing the white notes going up the keyboard CDEFGABC is the scale of C. It is called the diatonic or major scale – see fig 2.2. The five lines are called staves. Lines above or below these staves are called ledger lines. Middle C is placed on one of these lines, on both base and treble clefs. The bass scale will hardly be used.

---

[4] Symbolised C#

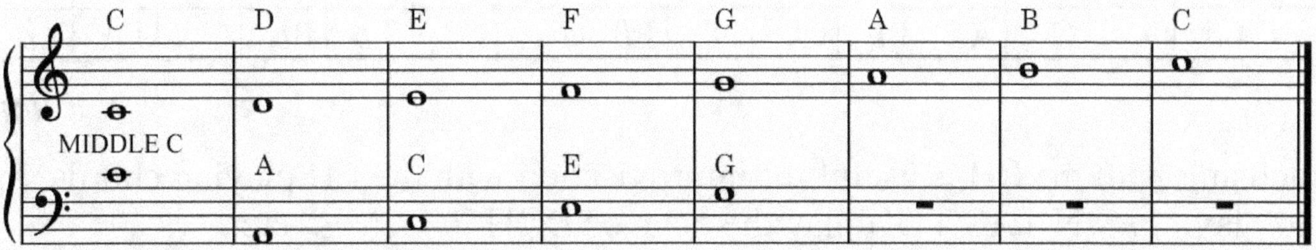

Fig 2.2

If the bass lines are moved up there are eleven lines.

See notes : F, A, C, E, going up the treble and A, C,E,G, on bass clef.

The differences in pitch between successive notes are whole tones (W) or half tones in the treble, (H). The major scale in C is CDEFGABC i.e CΔ7

Interval:- WWHWWWH. Note: 8 NOTES SEVEN INTERVALS.

When singers practice this scale, they sing the sound

DOH RAY ME FAH SO LA TE DOH

The sung sounds they make, bear relation to the whole tones and half tones.

Play the notes on the piano as you sing them.

There are five W's and 2H's in one octave in the above scale of C.

The fingering to play the C major scale is as follows:- Left and Right hands,

THUMB FINGER	INDEX FINGER	MIDDLE FINGER	THIRD FINGER	LITTLE FINGER
1	2	3	4	5

Fig 2.3A

RH	1	2	3	1	2	3	4	1	2	3	1	2	3	4	5
	C	D	E	F	G	A	B	C	D	E	F	G	A	B	C
LH	5	4	3	2	1	3	2	1	4	3	2	1	3	2	1

Fig 2.3B: Major scale in C

In both hands, 5 is the little finger, thumb is 1, play the two octaves using Left Hand (LH) then Right Hand (RH).

When you've got smooth execution try both hands together – separated by an octave. Check out the fingering in the scale below:- (on the Piano it is the scale of E♭.)

RH	2	1	2	3	4	1	2	3	1	2	3	4	1	2	3
	Eb	F	G	Ab	Bb	C	D	Eb	F	G	Ab	Bb	C	D	Eb

E flat.

Practising with the RH is useful for improvisation with the LH playing chords. In solo playing. SING AS YOU play the octave "DOH RAY ME" etc.

There are 3 flats in this scale: Eb, Ab and Bb. There 3 flats should be located at the beginning of the staves in Fig 2.5, by the student. First in pencil.

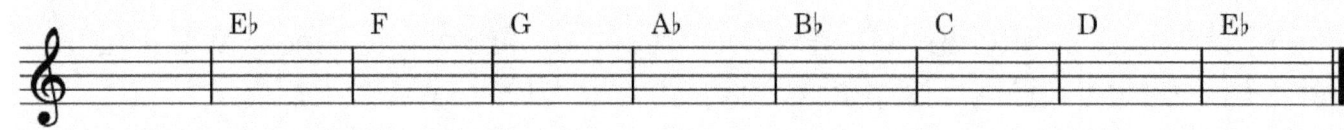

Fig 2.5

Write the scale in the stave above.

The song *"I'm Old Fashioned"* in 3 flats, the eight notes in Fig 2.5 conform in tones to (once more) WWHWWWH; these SEVEN intervals between Eb and Eb upper make one octave. 1 Octave = 5W + 2H = 12 semitones.

RH	2	1	2	3	1	2	3	4	1	2	3	1	2	3	4
	Bb	C	D	Eb	F	G	A	Bb	C	D	Eb	F	G	A	Bb
	3	2	1	4	3	2	1	3	2	1	4	3	2	1	2

Fig 2.6 Shows two octaves of Bb major

The scale with 2 flats is shown in fig 2.6. Major scale of F sharp is shown in the Fig 2.7. the circle of 5ths shows F sharp with 6 sharps. (Located at half past the hour)

F#	G#	A	B	C#	D#	E#	F#

Fig 2.7

Circle of 5ths in Fig 4.9 Chapter 4 shows 6 sharps, or Fig 4.1.

Note that there are only 5 black notes on the piano! A later section deals with the circle of fifths, chapter 4, which shows this anomaly. The number of sharps (or flats) goes up as one travels round the circle and progresses to six at 6'o'clock! Circle is shown in Fig 4.1 also.

In the glossary section, look up G for Gb (or F#)

The music sheet "*Lazy Bird*" by John Coltrane is written in one sharp. The Blue Train CD has tunes which are covered by sheets of music at Chapter 8.

RH	1	2	3	1				
	G	A	B	C	D	E	F#	G

Fig 2.8

Sit at the keyboard and write in your fingering for the remaining spaces. Notes in this scale are given. Sing the notes, they follow DOH RAY ME FAH SO LA TE DOH. Note the intervals: WWHWWWH. Note: 8 notes and 7 intervals (spaces and lamp posts)

Remember that the major scale has 5 whole tone intervals and two half (semi) tones in one octave. GO UP FROM G

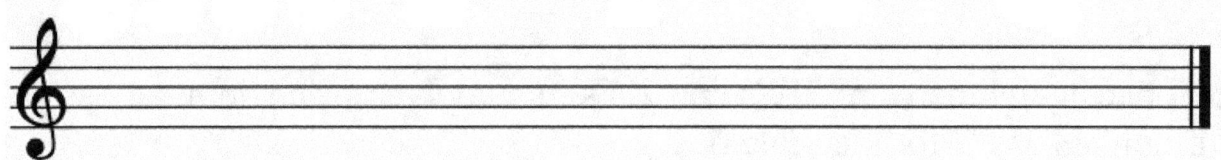

Write the dots in the treble scale (in pencil, in case of mistakes).

2.2 Minor Scales.

(-) is the symbol in this book. In Jazz, the minor scale is called the DORIAN minor scale and is best remembered by referring to the white notes on the piano for D Dorian Minor.

D-7 = D E F G A B C

Q2.2 Write scales, in letters for

(i) A-7

(ii) E♭-7 (seven letters in each answer)

Having written them, play the piano using them. HINT: REFER BACK TO D DORIAN MINOR SCALE AND NOTE WHERE THE W's AND H's ARE. USE THAT INFORMATION WITH THE SCALE OF E♭ MINOR. USE THE PIANO TO RAISE EACH OF THE WHITE NOTES OF D-7 ONE SEMI TONE. USE THE SPACE of Chapter nine. E♭ is one semitone above D. Write A minor after.

2.3. Dominant 7th SCALES

This scale is the major scale with one modification – the seventh note is flattened. The number seven in the last sentence needs explaining, it relates to the interval between a certain two notes – this needs defining. Intervals are measured by the number of letter names from the lower note to the upper, both of which are included in the count. Thus from C to D, there are only two letter names included, therefore this is an interval of a second (or two). From C up to B there are seven letter names: CDEFGAB, so C to B is an interval of a seventh. The definition of an interval needs an extra piece of information – major to minor. C to E is an interval of a major third (W+W). C to Eb is an interval of a minor third (W + H). So the flattened seventh note Bb is an interval of minor seventh from C. The scale of the dominant seventh of C is CDEFGABb = C7. Play these notes and write the intervals in W's and H's: - In advance of the next section, just play the two chords CEGB and CEGBb and compare the sound. There's a big difference.

(note, once again, there are 5W's and 2H's in an octave.) The dominant seventh is symbolized as C7 for the scale of C.

    Q2.3: Sit at piano, write and sing DO, RE…. For the major scales of

    (i) BbΔ7

    (ii) Db Δ7. These scales both have major 7th

    (iii) Write the scales of G7, D7

HINT: ONCE AGAIN PLAY THE SCALE YOU KNOW, i.e. C7, MANY TIMES. GET USED TO THE SOUNDS (YOU CAN ALWAYS CHECK THE ANSWER CH 9).

Note: D7 is one tone above C7.

(All answers are at the back of the book)

Chapter 3 - Chords

3.1 Major chords for solo

Naturally these chords are formed by the left hand and contain 4 notes. They can extend an octave below middle C. To play this chord 2 octave below C sounds a little "rough"!

3 (a)   CΔ7 = CEGB   C Major (As in Fig 3.1)

   CΔ6 = CEGA   (note interval of 6 to C to A)

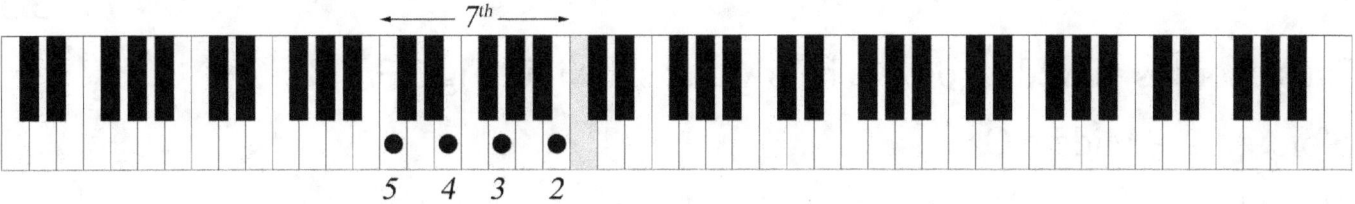

Fig 3.1

FINGERING   5   4   3   2 } CHOICE

                   5   3   2   1 }

Some books refer to the major scale as C maj., or C m or Cma or CMA. This book will use CΔ. Jamey Abersold uses CΔ. (Ref 2)

Left hand fingering for this chord is shown in Fig3.1. (Remember 5 is the little finger the fingering 5432).

3.2 Minor chords for solo

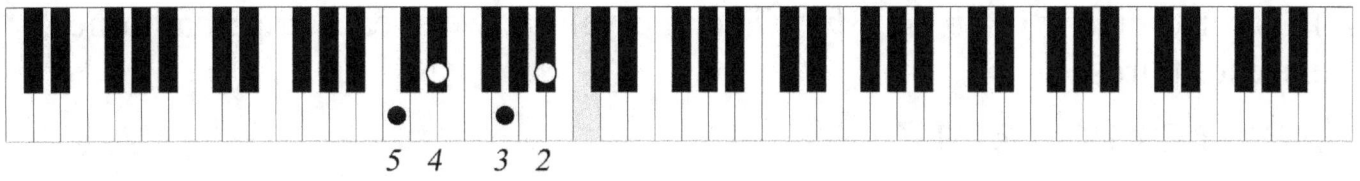

Fig 3.2

FINGERING, C MINOR

Refer back to 2.2 Minor Scales, D Dorian. Minor chord is D (W+H) F(W+W) A(W+H) C(All white notes). INSIDE THE BRACKETS ARE THE INTERVALS, SO D(W+H) IS A MINOR THIRD TO F ETC.

The intervals are shown above. These same intervals must be preserved in four note minor chords, So C Minor (shown in Fig, 3.2) is therefore:-

C E♭ G B♭ = A four finger chord with the three following intervals:-

Minor Third   Major Third   Minor Third

i.e. Four notes three intervals.

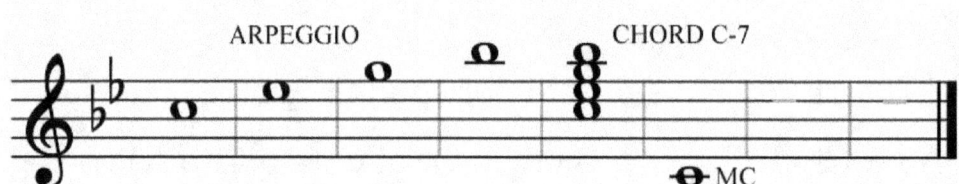

Fig 3.3

This chord is played an octave below that shown in Fig 3.3

Note: MC = Middle C.

Note: With respect to the minor major, the chord: - C – Δ7, this chord has a minor third (E♭) and a major seventh (B). The subject of timing will be dealt with in a separate section, but in Fig 3.3 the notes are played as a chord. This means that they are played together. Timing: See glossary, under T.

3.3 C7= CEGB♭ Dominant seventh.

These are minor sevenths.

It is a major chord with flattened 7th. See glossary under D for DOMINANT.

Q3.3 Write the series of notes constituting G♭7

3.4 Other chords (SOLO)

(i) Co (or C dim) = C E♭ G♭ B♭ A. The intervals between each are 3 half tones, i.e. minor thirds

(ii) C+ or C AUG 5 is C E G# C.

(iii) CΦ is half diminished, C E♭ G♭ B♭

(iv) PENTANTONIC CHORDS AND SCALES

In key C three chords form the basis.

Major: CEG, FAC and GBD. The arrangement of the notes in each chord are the same. The intervals are 2W and 1½W (Three notes – two intervals)

Minor: C E♭ G, F A♭ C, G B♭ D. Intervals are 1½ W and 2W.

The scales, written for an octave has six notes. Easiest to remember, it uses only the black notes, G♭ to G♭ (NOT G♭Δ7) G♭ Major FIG 3.4. In the key of C the notes are: C D E G A C. The minor pentatonic scale is C E♭ F G B♭ C.

The above pentatonic scales and chords will be used in the section on improvisation. Fig 3.4 shows the pentatonic major scale in C. Also shown is the scale for G♭. (i.e. the black notes – G♭ major pentatonic)

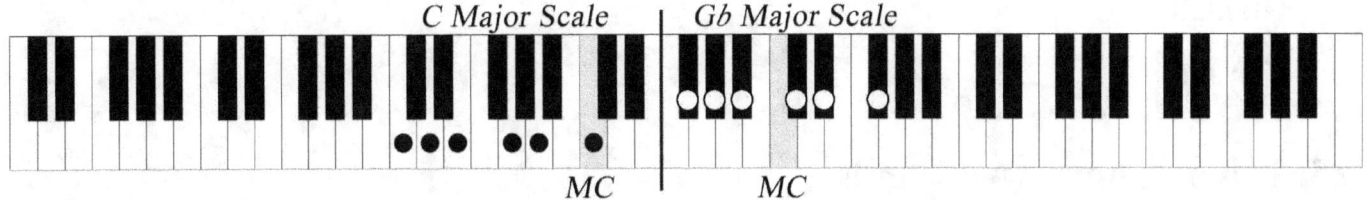

Fig 3.4

3.5 Chords for band pianists.

Band pianists devote both hands to play the chord. The LH plays two notes only, separated by an octave (root of chord). The RH plays third, fifth and seventh. This, of course, gives a better spread of the notes (4 octaves in the case shown below). The RH can be played an octave below that shown; that sounds even better. (It does to me anyway!)

3.5b /c major CΔ7 ninth is optional

Notes shown C C   EGBD symbolised CΔ9

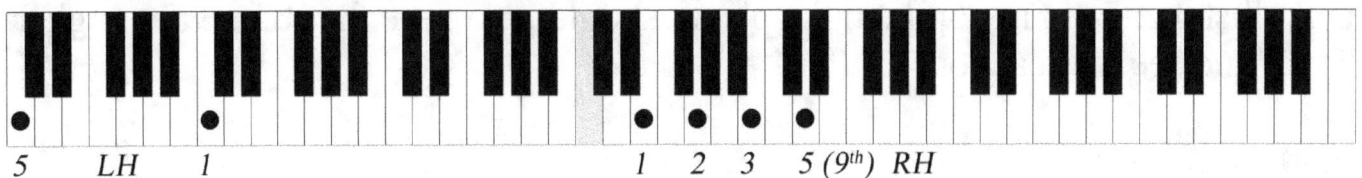

Fig 3.5a

A ninth has been included (optional). The positioning of LH notes can be raised by one octave. In the set up in Fig 3.5a, the two wrists are about 15 inches (38cm) apart.

So that you may start your playing in a band with the wrists separated by a lower value than Fig 3.5a. As you improve, the LH may move down the piano first by one octave and then by two octaves. The latter must always be the final aim. The aim in all band accompaniment is to get the widest range possible. Big bands sound best when there are baritone and soprano saxes present. There are many variations in the CΔ7 (see reference 4 and 3.1a).

Q 3.4 By playing the piano and listening, write out the key notes of the following chords.

(i) AbΔ

(ii) Gb7

(iii) EΦ

(iv) CΦ

3.5c Minor Chord Two Hands

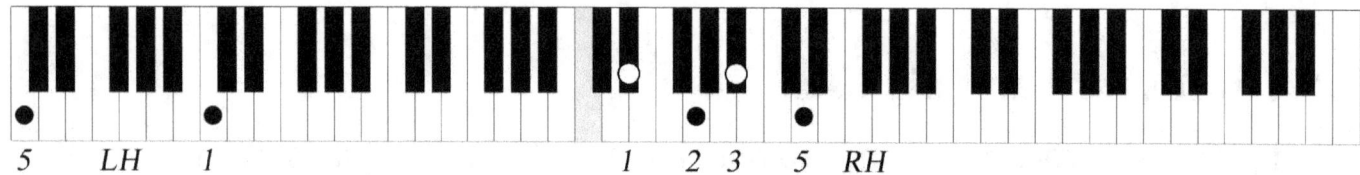

Fig 3.5b

[LH]CC   [RH]EbGBb is the chord C-7.

The further down the piano that the root C can be played, the bigger the frequency range. The confidence of the player improves with experience. A person just starting a band accompaniment will inevitably play the root higher up. The D (ninth) at the upper end of the chord can be added, but it is of prime importance that the chord is played on time rather than attempting embellishments. In my opinion the player should not move the RH up any higher. Try it and see the reaction!

3.5d Dominant 7th

The facility to embellish this chord is almost limitless. However the more complicated the chord, the timing can suffer. This is the restriction that is placed upon the band player. It's OK with soloing, in the absence of a bass player and any others. Audiences do not notice a slight departure from the written music, whether in time or in selection of notes.

The dominant 7th chord is the major chord with a flattened 7th. With the LH covering the root as with the two previous types of chords (3.2b and 3.1b)

[LH]CC   [RH]EGBb is the chord C7

An interesting variation is shown below in Fig 3.6

Just check the note at the 11th Symbolised C11 (b9)

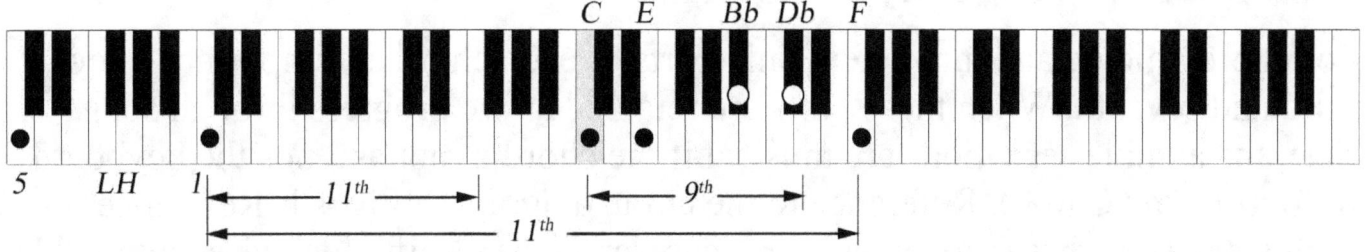

Fig 3.6

The root C,E, and B*b* are retained, the F is an 11th from the root, and D*b* is a flattened ninth.

The major 3rd is included. You wouldn't play this chord instantly.

Questions on 3b: This section is very similar to 3a, except the root part and certain extensions in the RH, such as 9ths and 11ths.

Q3.5 Write the notes in the following chords:

(i) FΔ7+5

(ii) B*b*7 (Two handed chord, remember)

(iii) D*b*o

(iv) F13(b9)

Two handed chords, LH and RH. Not solo.

Chapter 4 - Circle of Fifths

For chord voicing and movement only parts of each chord are important – root, third and seventh. When these parts are retained as we progress through song/tune, the audible sensations are musical if the chord's root ascends the keyboard in fourths (ex: C to F). Reference to the circle diagram in Fig 4.1. Reference to this diagram, these movements are represented as a shift clockwise from 12 o'clock to 5 minutes past, which is highly convenient on the clock face. There are twelve positions for the minutes (60 divided by 5) finger. They go 12 o'clock, five past, ten past etc.

NB See Fig 2.7 CH 2 – 6 Sharps in the Scale of F# and G*b*. *G* Major has 1 sharp, F Major has 1 flat etc.

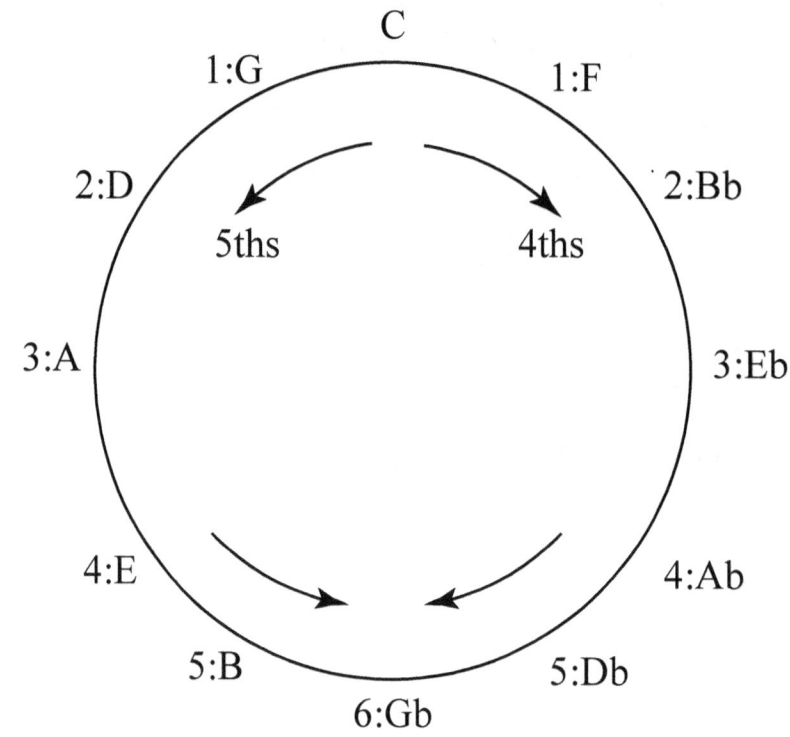

Fig 4.1

The movement of chord roots up in fourths or down in fifths along the keyboard can be seen in the music of (i) "*Moments Notice*" and (ii) "*Lazy Bird*". Also there are many cases of two chords in one bar, and bearing in mind the speed of these two pieces of music, the finger movement is going to have to be somehow simplified, If that's possible. In fact in (i), It is apparent there are around fifteen bars containing pairs of chords that are minor followed by dominant 7th. Some of them are followed by a major chord: Each pair are formed of root notes separated by a fifth. The Minor chord is a "sad" chord, the dominant 7th is a step towards "brightness". A further step in brightening is the major chord. These three chords are members of the II V I sequence. The Roman Numerals in this case refer to their position of the Piano scales. So ABCDEFGA (8 notes) is represented as I

II III IV V VI VII (or I) (one octave, octo = 8). These Roman Numerals are used purely for their relative positions. II V I applies to cadences in any key.

So II V I equates to DGC:- three successive positions on the clock face. The movement from "sad" toward brightness (listed as you play D-7 to G7) as the player moves from minor to dominant 7th, you may consider this is so.

D-7 is (i) D F A C

G7 is (ii) G B D F. But this chord is now inverted. i.e. (iii) D F G B (also equal to G7)

Finally (iv) C E G B (This is C∆, C Major).

So play LH (i) then (iii) and then (iv). This is D-7 G7 C∆. Three positions on the cycle of the fifths. Sadness to brightness by fifths ensures their musicality, as already stated. We say that chord (i) resolves to (iii) and then to (iv). It only remains for you to be trained to make movements (i) to (iii) easily, and quickly. This training will be now carried out. It is a very simple movement of two fingers.

The movement is shown below: - Refer to the fingering of the LH in Fig 2.3

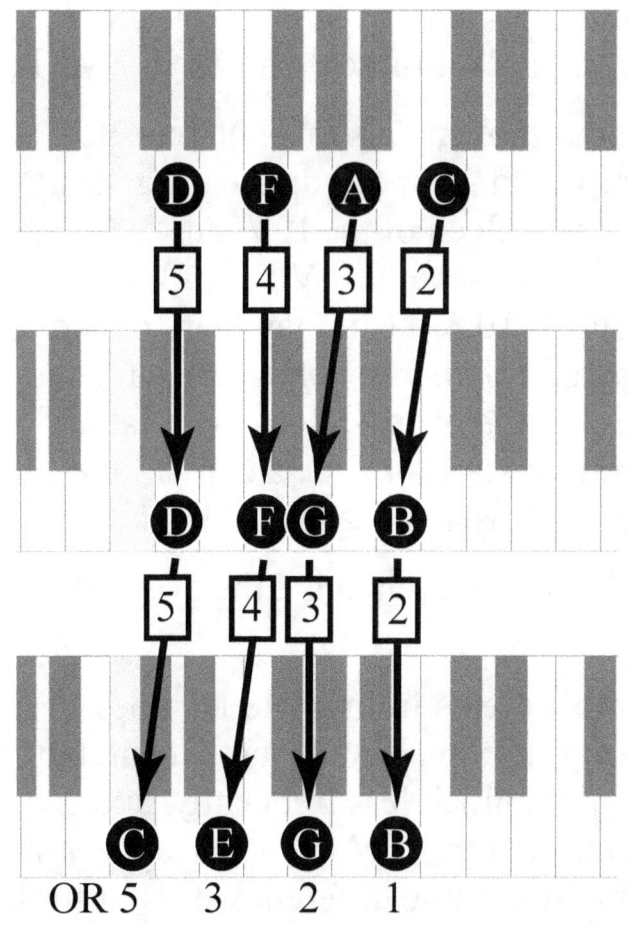

Fig 4.2

In the first transition,

    A goes to G (Finger 3)

    C goes to B (Finger 2)

    Chord DFAC →DFGB →CEGB

This minor → dom 7th → major is possible in all 12 keys but is used in a much smaller no. of keys.

The movement in Fig4.2 is using only white (natural) notes, and from this two diagram you can see that finger 2 moves down one half (H) or a semitone, from C to B. Finger 3 moves down one tone, from A to G. This rule must be remembered, and adhered to when you meet sharps.

Let us continue using this rule with the first bar of "*Moment's Notice*".

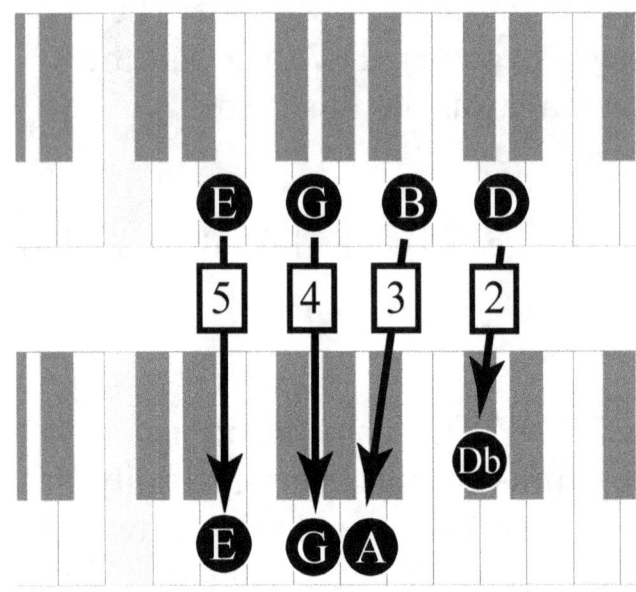

Fig 4.3

The note D falls by a semitone to D*b*. The note B falls by a tone to A (Finger 3). See this movement in Figs 4.3 and 4.4. Only the two fingers, index and middle (2 and 3) move (see the two arrows) and no wrist movement in this change from E-7 to A7.

Bars 10 and 11 in the tune show that E*b*-7 → A*b*7 moves to D*b*Δ7.

D*b* Δ7 = D*b* F A*b* C. Study Fig 4.4 which shows the two chord and their fingering.

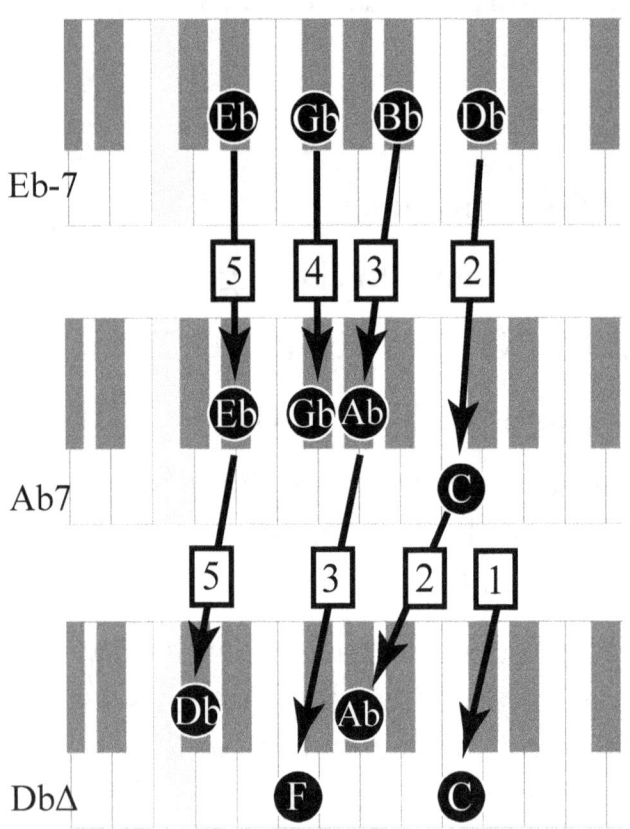

Fig 4.4

Try this out on the piano. Get used to the three sounds for these 3 chords II-7 V7 IΔ

All those movements must be repeated and repeated, to speed up the progression. There are fifteen of the II V's in "*Moments Notice*", and several II V I's in Bars 2 & 3, 6 and 7, 10 & 11. It may help to take a copy of "*Moments Notice*", to save the turning of the pages. (Books can fall off K/B music stands). Take a copy of the cycle of fifths also (saves the book too!)

Check these movements I the cycle of fifths.

The movements from V7 to IΔ, does require some small wrist movement, but it is required much less frequently, and is in a second bar. I repeat here that the II V cadence and the II V I cadence appear so often Jazz (30's, 40's & 50's) they represent (using some different words) a stress chord minor resolving into less and less stress (V and IΔ). Play notes one octave up in the song below. They also move in fifths and can add musicality (treble).

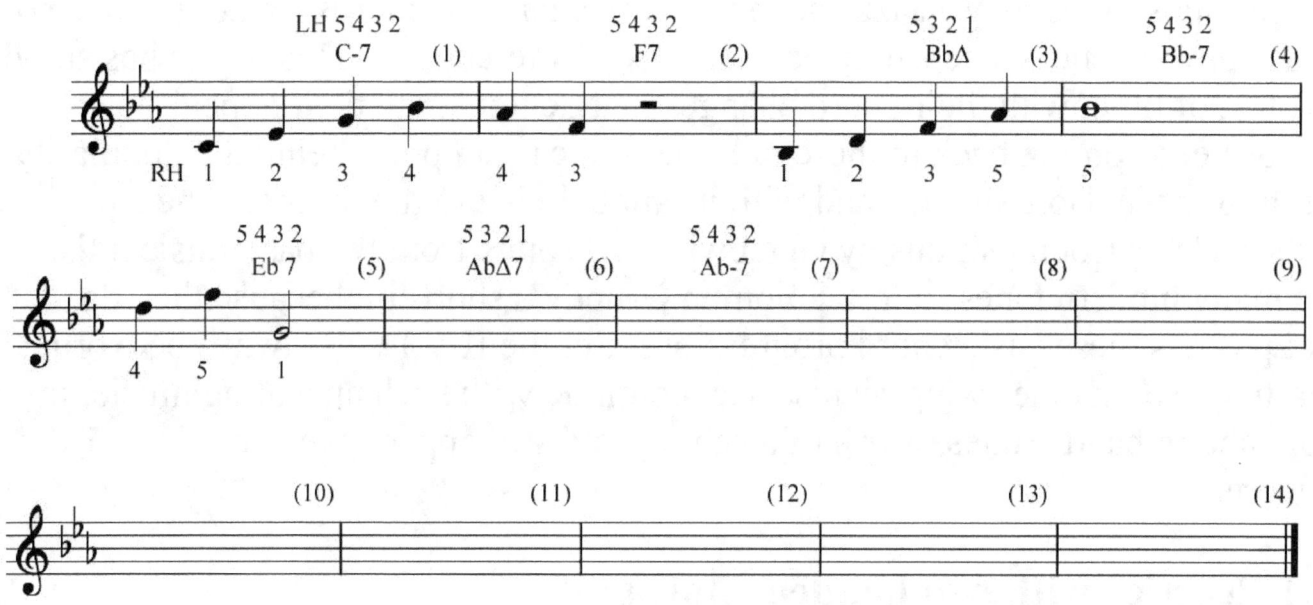

Fig 4.5

For timing of notes and rests see in glossary under T.

In Fig 4.5 B*b* ∆ changes to B*b*-7 and we continue to go round the clock to A*b* ∆ then A*b*-7 to ??? so compose a few bars of melody in space left.

In this song the melody is played one octave up[5] (RH). The chords are played above and below middle C (LH). So, complete the song using the above criteria.

Simply writing roots, thirds and sevenths relating to each chord is a first step.

You play the chords with the LH and the melody with the right hand. Some are half notes, so only two notes in a bar and you will note that in bar 4 you play B*b* as a semi breve. (See glossary under N and under T for timing).

Some years ago a Jazz class that I met weekly asked for volunteers to compose a tune to be played weeks later. I (the author) volunteered! The title of the tune was "*Round the Clock on the 251*". Parts to be written for sax, clarinette, piano, etc. So sheets of music were written (see glossary for saxes) in C (for Piano), E*b* and B*b*. So instrumentalists were playing the same notes as the pianist. All through the tune – it was a watery flop as if you are playing the tune with one finger, it is boring to listen to. That's why chords have been invented. Arrangers design music in different keys for different parts. So then each note in the tune is being replaced by a series of notes – say C, E, G, B*b* etc. Saxophones may play C, trombones play a lower B*b*. Then it begins to sound more musical. This same procedure is adopted by choirs. A chord formed of middle C and a Second C one octave[6] up would sound watery. Still on the subject of arranging music,

---

5   8ve means play one octave up, to avoid clash of hands.
6   8ve means play one octave up,

Jazz standards written in 30's, 40's 50's contain common aspects – turnarounds, tritone substitutes, II V I Jazz cadences, movements of chords round the cycle of 5th, happy cadences steeped in Harmony (see Reference 9). This music has stood the test of time, with their chord changes that demonstrate their appeal. Jazz bands keep coming back to these old titles – a case in point being the popularity of the John Wilson Swing Band with its annual visit to the proms at the Royal Albert Hall[7]. Compositions by Gershwin, and songs from the past musical lists. So many modern tunes follow Solomon Grundy's short life because they do not possess these basic chord progressions. So, the II V I will always be worth learning, so that the swing pianists can continue with such appealing music; in solo and in band. Tunes over half a century old still appear every week on TV adverts.

4.1 Practice with two handed chords.

The exercise of going round the clock with two handed chords, copies of 18 keyboards shown on the following pages Fig 4.10 (1-18) may be a little frightening. So let us revise the work leading up to those K/B pictures. We start with C-7 LH, as shown in Fig 4.6. The D note is optional. Fig 4.7 shows the standard move for LH. We now use RH in figs 4.8a and 4.8b. The roots for these RH Figs are now shifted to base. See Figs 4.10 (1) and (2)

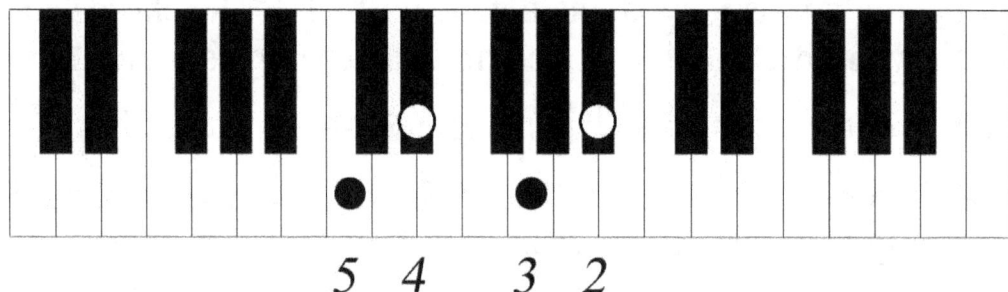

LH Fig 4.6 C – 7

Solo, one-handed chord

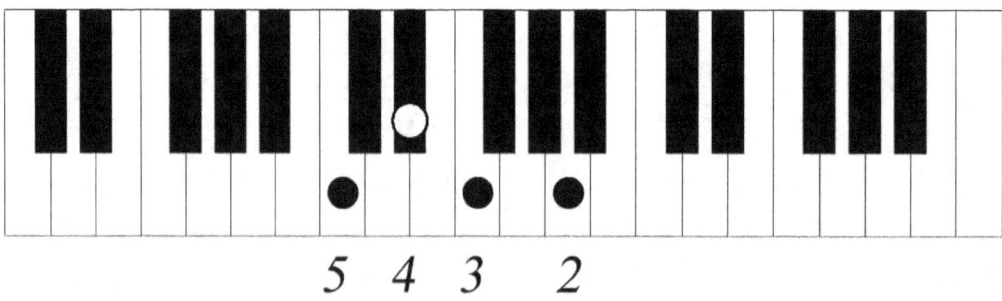

LH Fig 4.7

Solo

---
[7] London, England.

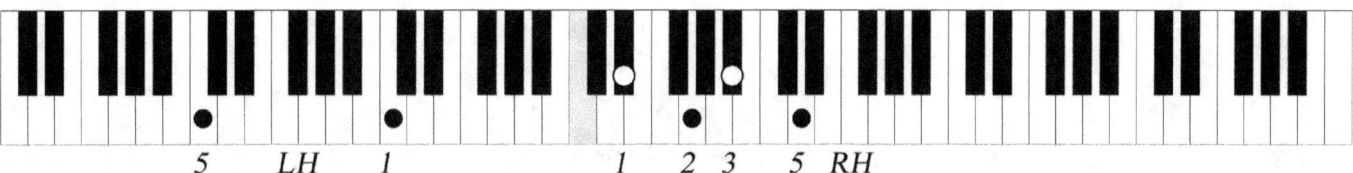

RH Fig 4.8(a) Double handed chord C-7.

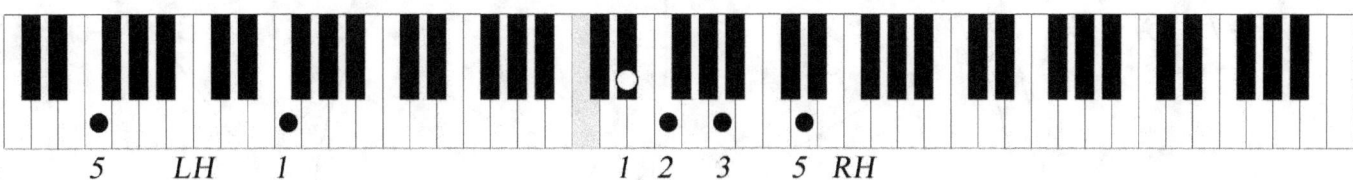

LH, RH Fig 4.8(b) F-7

Finger 5 is optional

Compare Figs 4.8a& b with Figs 4.10(1) and 4.10(2)

This exercise is to some extent musical; of course, it is if you are going round the cycle of fifths. The movements are appealing, and should be sufficiently attractive to make you want to repeat. Of course, if you wish you can go round the clock with LH only, (Figs 4.6 & 4.7) i.e. 4 note chords, this would be ideal preparations for a soloist. Having established this last procedure and got better at it, you introduce RH broken chords. Your LH will accompany your RH. Once such a procedure becomes fairly smooth, it becomes attractive and consequently enjoyable. And therefore irresistible to repeat and repeat. Complete mastery of the two-handed chords makes for an irreplaceable position as a Jazz band pianist.

Just in case you're perplexed by Fig 4.9, you're travelling round the circle of fifths. There are three ways of doing this, but starting at the top, you have seen in Figs 4.6, 4.7, 4.8(a) and (b) how it starts.

You reach BbΔ(3) then change to Bb – 7 (4). The number 4 tells you the particular K/B picture, i.e. Fig 5.0(4). This is that start of the second II – 7, V7 IΔ cadence. Each of the six cadences, shown in Fig 4.9, is a self-standing entity. As you play (albeit slowly at first) through the 18 K/B pictures, you'll find it's musicality improves, so attracting you to improve your continuity and speed. You will eventually get to know, and remember the order of these six cadences. These are all chords. They're RH chords with LH roots. As stated in the first paragraph after Fig 4.9, you can return to LH chords and RH improvisation. If you're keen to start improvising and not lumber yourself with two hand chords, you then refer to the single-handed chords (which was started in Figs 4.6 and 4.7)

4.2 "Round the Clock on the 251"

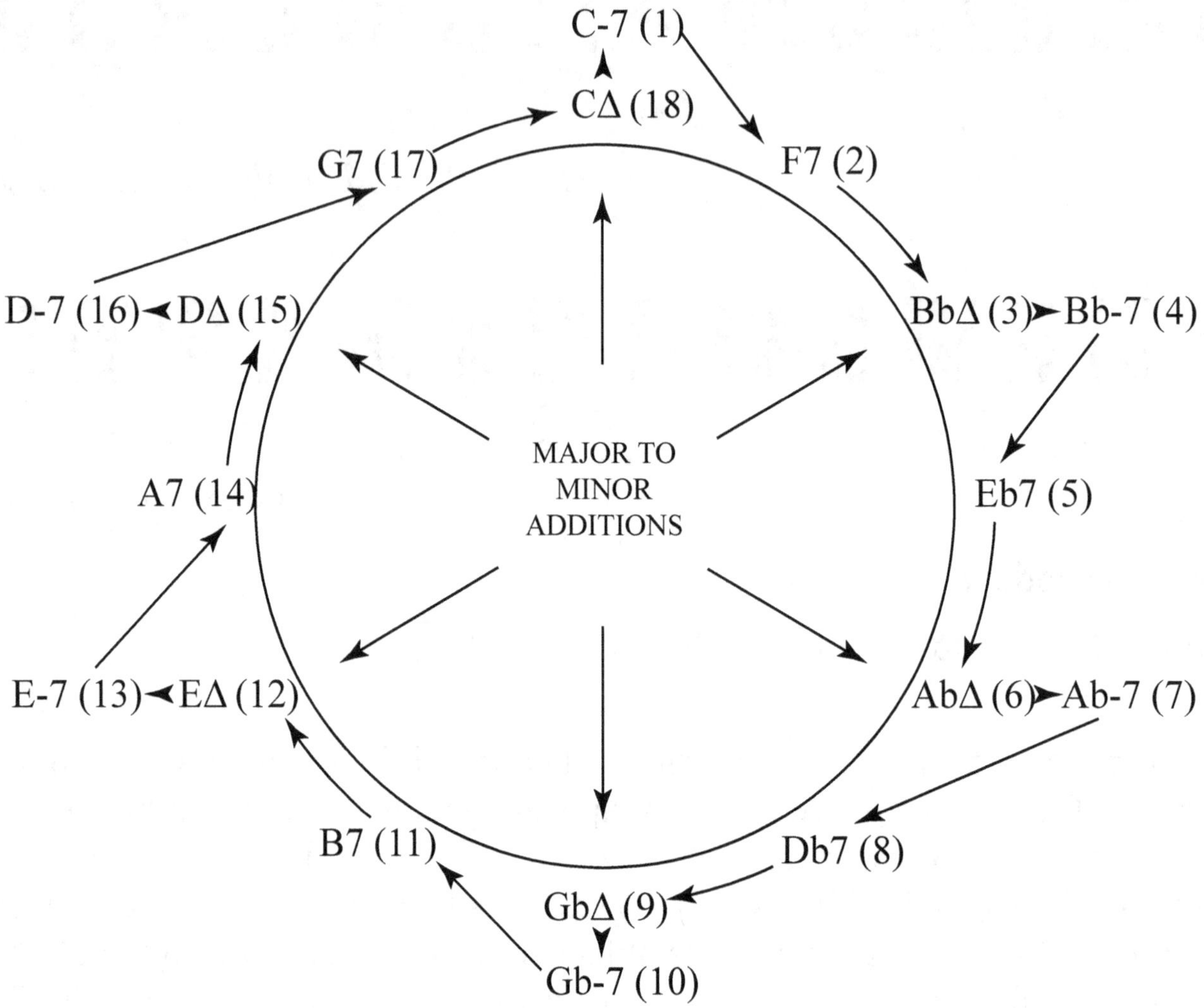

```
            C-7 (1)
         CΔ (18)
    G7 (17)          F7 (2)

D-7 (16)◄ DΔ (15)         BbΔ (3)► Bb-7 (4)

  A7 (14)      MAJOR TO       Eb7 (5)
                MINOR
               ADDITIONS

E-7 (13)◄ EΔ (12)         AbΔ (6)► Ab-7 (7)

    B7 (11)          Db7 (8)
         GbΔ (9)
         Gb-7 (10)
```

Fig 4.9

4.3 Exercise going 'round the clock' using both hands for the chord playing.

Exercise going round the clock using LH chords and RH broken chords or improvised notes, can be considered a jazz tune to play anytime, anywhere, including a hotel lounge or restaurant!

All chords in Fig 4.10(a-s) taken from Fig 4.9

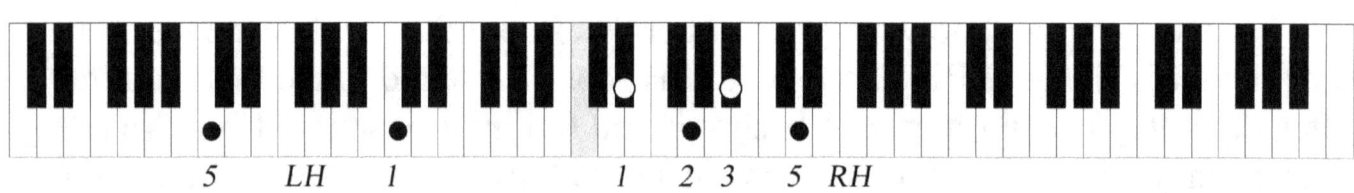

Fig 4.10(a) C – 7

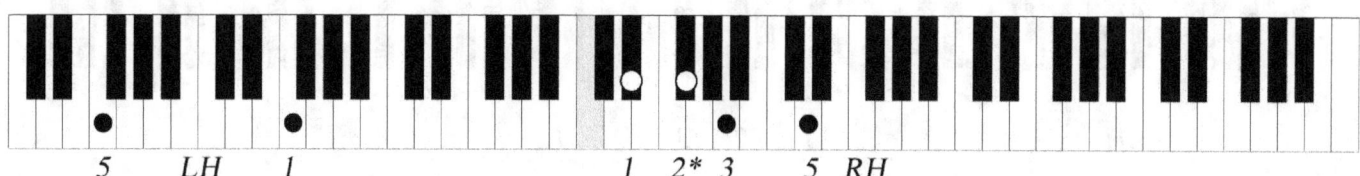

Fig 4.10(b) F7 (b9)

* $b9^{th}$ is easier than 8th

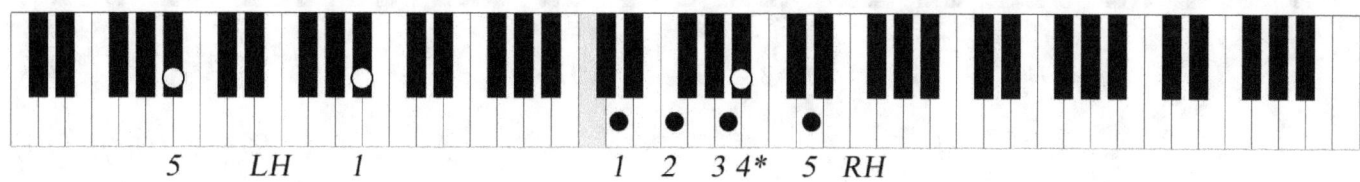

Fig 4.10(c) Bb∆

* Finger 4 is optional.

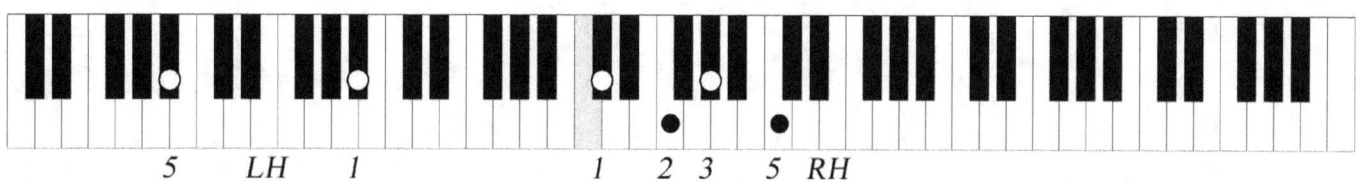

Fig 4.10(d) Bb–7

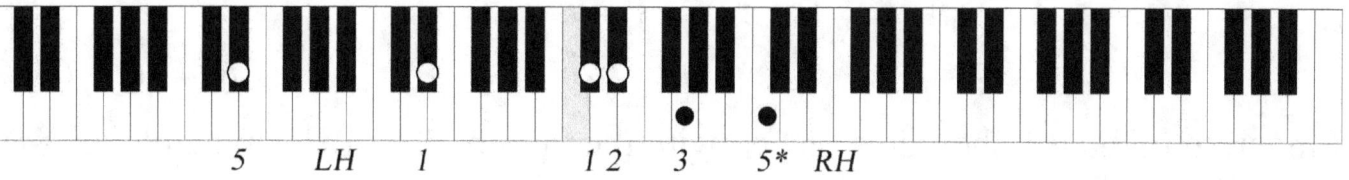

Fig 4.10(e) Eb7

* Finger 5 is optional.

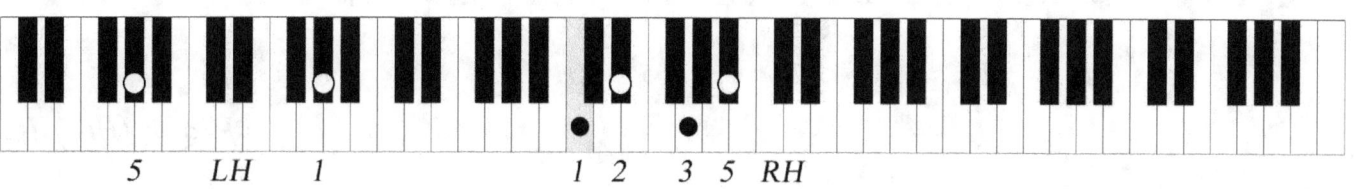

Fig 4.10(f) Ab∆

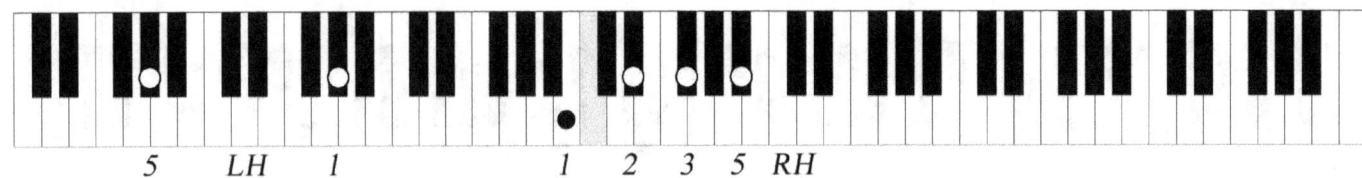

Fig 4.10(g) Ab-7

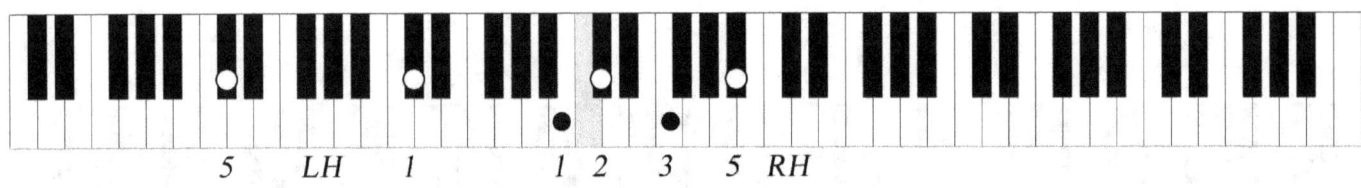

Fig 4.10(h) Db7

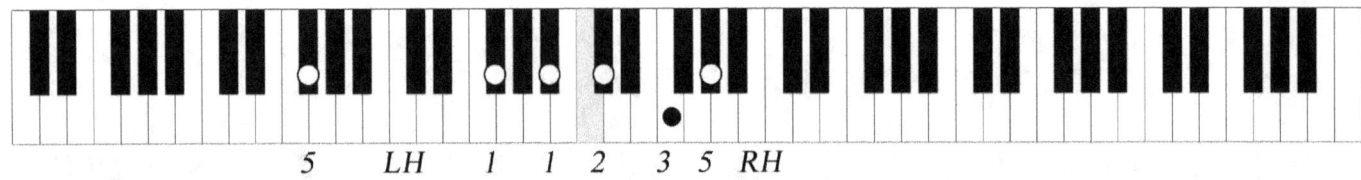

Fig 4.10(9) GbΔ7

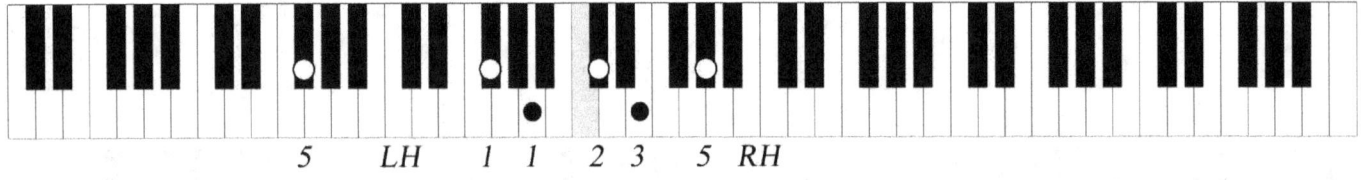

Fig 4.10(j) Gb-7

Fingering marked 1 should be played with the thumbs. The LH can be played 8va down if you wish.

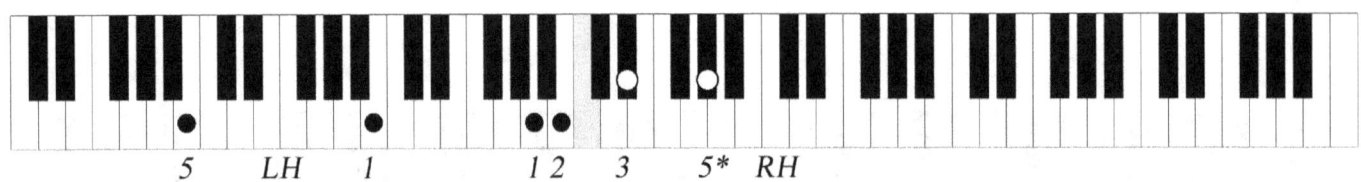

Fig 4.10(k) B7

* Finger 5 is optional.

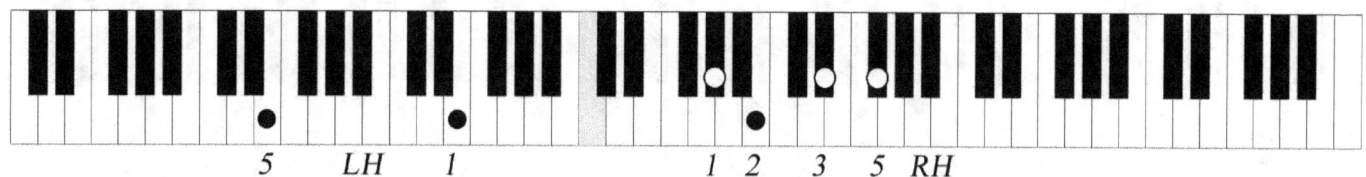

Fig 4.10(l) EΔ7

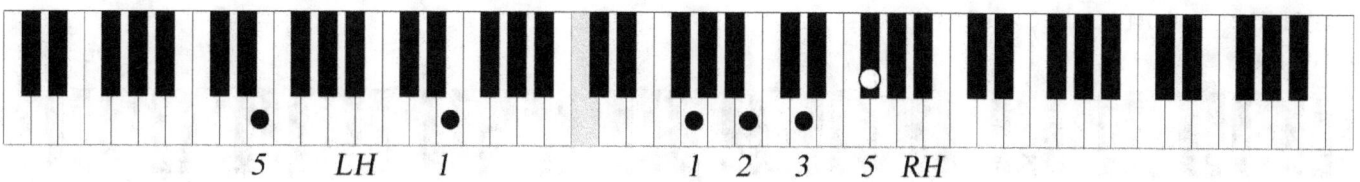

Fig 4.10(m) E – 7

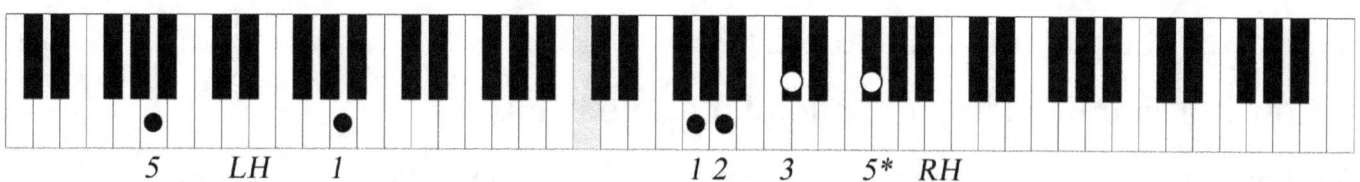

Fig 4.10(n) A7

* Finger 5 is optional.

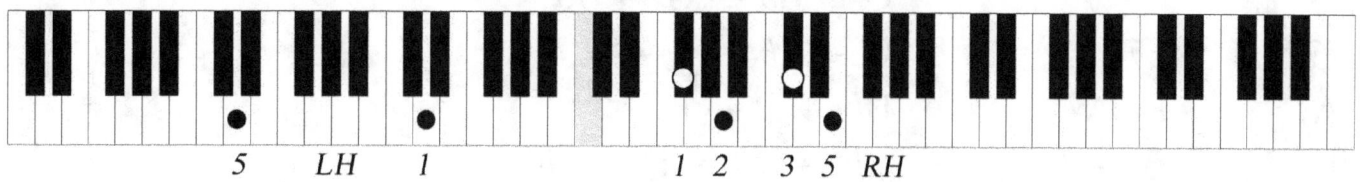

Fig 4.10(o) DΔ7

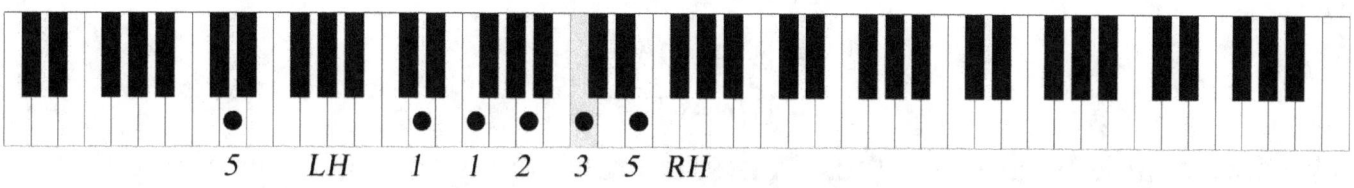

Fig 4.10(p) D–7 Dorian Minon: All white notes

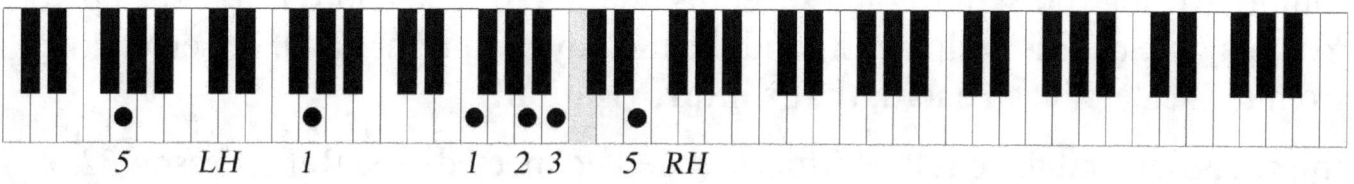

Fig 4.10(q) G7 All white notes

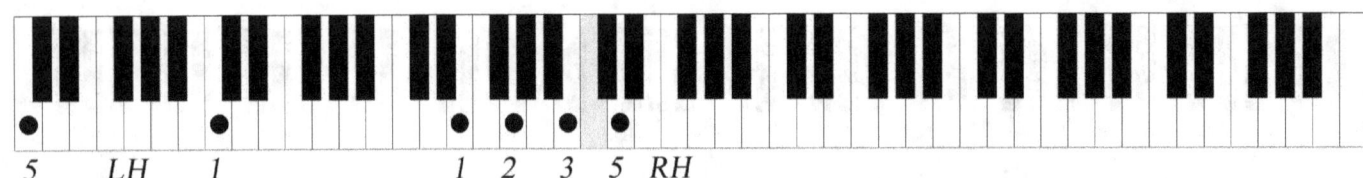

Fig 4.10(r) CΔ This completes the clock

This Major chord is now modified to its minor, ready to commence a new "journey" round the clock.

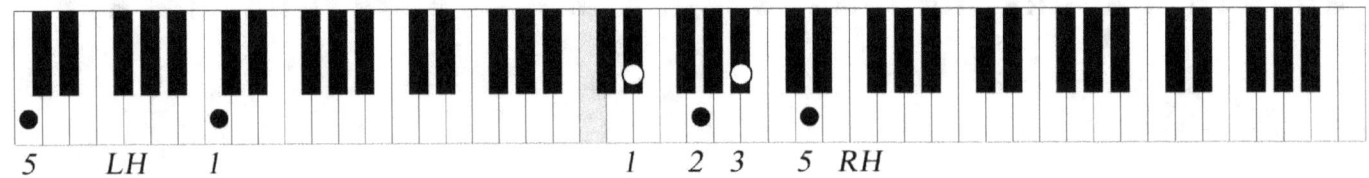

Fig 4.10(s) C–7

The lower you play the LH, the better!

Below is a simplified improvisation for a solo pianist.

Rather than using K/B pictures for these single handed, the notes are played in order, going up the K/B scale. Starting at the top of the clock with C-7 (cadence chord). Notes starting with root.

LH (5421)		RH (1235)
II – 7	C – 7	C → E♭ → G → B♭
V7	F7	C → E♭ → F → A
IΔ7	B♭ Δ7	B♭ → D → F → A
II – 7	B♭ – 7	B♭ → D♭ → F → A♭
V7	E♭ 7	B♭ → D♭ → E♭ → G
IΔ7	A♭ Δ7	A♭ → C → E♭ → G
II – 7	A♭ – 7	A♭ → B → E♭ → F#
V7	D♭7	A♭ → B → D♭ → F
IΔ7	G♭Δ7	G♭ → B♭ → D♭ → F

The above table is half the clock. A first exercise using this table is to play the chord (LH) and arpeggio through the notes (RH). We say that the RH is playing the broken chords. If you know the scale you can play the scale (RH).

Simply writing roots, thirds and sevenths relating to each chord is a first step. You play the chords with the LH and the melody with right hand, or select notes from the scale of each chord; **that's improvisation!**

Improvisaion and the circle of fifths are well connected. See Ref 9, lesson 62, where John Mehegan takes both subjects to a higher level.

Chapter 5 - Playing along

5.1 Playing the four pieces of music using your CD.

The John Coltrane pieces are of course faster than the "*I'm Old Fashioned*" piece.

This makes the latter the preferred first one, for first practise using the II V I cadence.

But there are four pieces, and it's best for you to choose.

a) "*Moment's Notice*"

Harder than (b), it's faster. This music sheet only covers the first 21 bars. This is a good exercise for using the II V I cadence (and the shortened much more frequently encountered II V 7). Practise of course improves the speed of execution. There are other bass chords – bars 15 & 16 with an unrelated chord in each (i.e not II V's). These take longer to play, which just go to show the advantage of the quick movement II V's executions. Strict time is not adhered to in this piece. Though every attempt has been made to include every note playing along with the CD, you'll be doing very well. This piece "*Moment's Notice*" is played through first by Coltrane, playing the tune, then more than once he is improvising, then improvisations with Trombone, then Trumpet, then bass player (bowed), piano player[8] and finally the band. When any of these instrumentalists is playing, you, the pianist could attempt to play the chords only, using one hand (LH). This is very difficult with this piece as it will be your first or second attempt – reading the chords and playing them in time. Also, the soloists include several executions of the piece.

b) "*I'm Old Fashioned*"

This tune is a **MUST** for your first attempt at playing the piano along with other instrumentalists in the CD. The melody is written one octave up on the INTRO, to leave room for LH chords.

First there's an introduction by the pianist. This is a fairly slow piece (with an intro first) and you can play along with the CD, using the music provided. This is good for those students still learning notes in the treble clef. Next Coltrane plays the piece, and here you can play – first the top line (treble) – all single notes, with him (on his sax). You'll get to know the tune after a few repeats, if you don't already know it. You'll make mistakes, so you start again. Start the CD off again from the beginning and this time when Coltrane plays the tune you accompany him with just the chords (LH only at first) as outlined in the music sheet. Again

---

8   See reference 2. Abersold is good for timing.

you will make mistakes. Improvisors take over at this point, first trombone, then piano, then trumpet. With each of these improvisors you can play the chords outlined in the music. You will lose your place in the music or you'll play too fast or too slow, each time, you stop the music and start again. If accompanying with chords you can choose the simple one hand (LH), four notes each chord, for a start. As you get better you can choose two hand chords. All this practice is good for you. Nobody is listening to you, so you can make mistakes and start again. Don't join a band too early otherwise you suffer the embarrassment of people laughing at you. Bands will expect two hand chords, so be warned!

For many piano students, who have a great responsibility in a band, you have to keep time, the saxes, the bassoon, trumpets, rely on you, and also quite possibly the bass player (assuming this player plays the right notes at the right time). You can get further experience playing with a rhythm section music, with music sheets provided. To that end Jamey Abersold, an American company has done a huge number of music books and accompanying CDs for the amateur. These are obtainable from music shops. The contact number etc is in the references at the back of this book. An alternative is to choose a new CD (a slow one) from a music shop, and find a "Real Book of Jazz", with specified chords, not with bass clef, with a few hundred pages of music including the titles of music in your new CD. Occasionally the music sheet may not be in the same key, so you have to transpose the music. This applies to the present song "*I'm Old Fashioned*", and "*Blue Trane*" they were in different keys to the CD, so I've had to transpose the songs. The CD for this book is obtainable from Amazon or a large CD shop[9]. I may well do another group of songs with music sheets. The only difficulty is with copyright; I do my own sheets. The reference number and title of the CD for this book are listed under References at the end of the book.

If you propose to play piano in a band with (LH & RH) chords:-

I have just one other point regarding playing this music. It is in regard to timing[10], i.e playing the chords in the music sheet on time. Hopefully you can reproduce chords quick enough, but you might find that you are still getting the timing wrong. You must resort to repeating 1 2 3 4 for every bar and you will of course find it monotonous, but you can test this repeating 1 2 3 4 without the chords, through the complete piece (often 32 bars) as an instrumentalist is performing his improvisation or playing the actual tune. Did you finish your counting at the same instant as the soloist performed his improvisation or playing the actual tune. Did you finish your counting at the same instant that the performer finished the tune? Sometimes there's a silence of one or two beats because the musician has done his homework & he finishes on time. Some appear to have a "built in clock", and we should be envious of them.

---

9   see reference 2
10   See glossary under G for Guitar for hints on timing.

c) "Lazy Bird"

INTRO: The roll of four quaver notes is played eight times in total as shown. Then two chords: - (each A*b*, B, E*b*, F) are played (staccato – see glossary) in quick succession. Then a trumpet plays the actual tune.

Referring to the script you play the first eight bars to the sign ':'[11] Go back to beginning and play next eight bars (That's a standard 16 bars). Go to bar 17, play to bar 24: go back to the head and play to + (Hot cross bun)(bar 7). Then go to bar 32 (the second +) and play the remaining 11 bars. The chord diagram is a standard way of writing tunes using only chords, see reference 6. No melody. It is suggested you play with RH the melody with the trumpeter a few times. Then play the chords with the trumpeter a few times. The last 11 bars (blocks C & D) are of less importance for this exercise.

For D*b*7, the last chord, play upper G for #11.

d) "Blue Trane"

FLATS B*b*, D*b* E*b* A*b* (FOUR). What key is this in?

To play this tune solo, you'll find the LH & RH fairly close together. A*b* – 7 uses four fingers with the first two 5 and 4 on the A*b* and B natural, just below middle C. The RH will start the treble with B*b* (Staccato – see glossary[12]). Treble notes can differ from CD version by an octave to avoid a hand clash.

The flats in the figure are B*b*, D*b*, E*b*, A*b*, G*b* as before. Music for this title show one bass chord type in every other bar 1, 3, 5, etc. The *Blue Trane* CD produces a drum sound (accompanied by piano) which has two staccato chords timed as shown in the figure below, signified by a dot over each chord. In the INTRO the Treble D*b*s coincide with two bass chords. Repeat this timing through the tune. NOTE THE CADENCES II-7 V7 IΔ6 in BARS 2&3, & 4&5. NOTE II V cadence in bar 8.

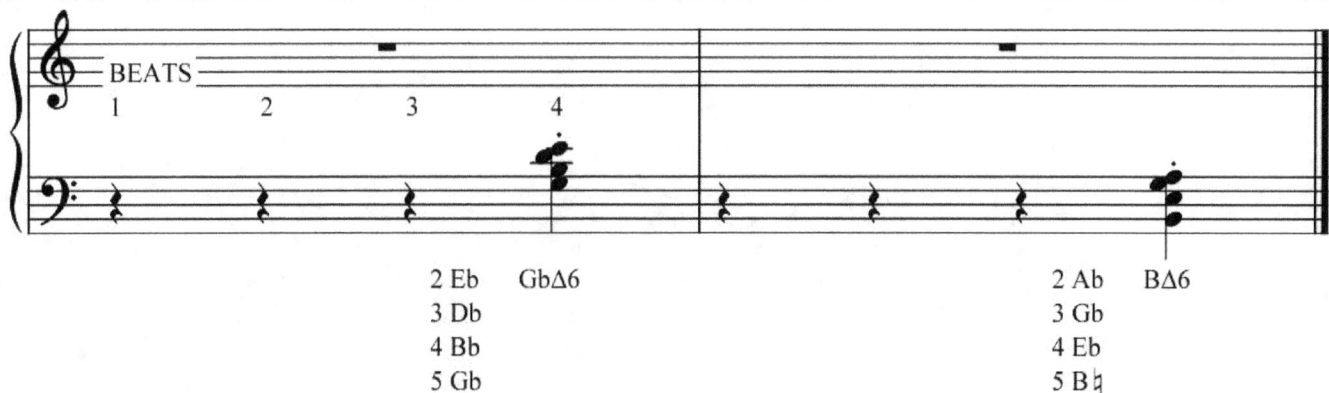

Those two staccato notes are occupying the second half of bars 1, 3, 5, etc. The

---

11   ':' is DC – see glossary
12   Staccato chords have a dot over the chord G*b*6, or a wedge shape ot dot above the notes (LAZY BIRD).

timing of the other chords are shown in this figure. Staccato chords are also in Lazy Bird, piano in the last bar of INTRO. It is difficult to compare these two very different staccatos, and the duration of each; this aspect is addressed in the glossary. LH fingers 5, 4, 3, 2 or 5, 3, 2, 1 play G♭6 – 4 black notes makes for easier improvisation.

Chapter 6 - Inprovisation

After playing the whole melody (so often 32 bars), improvisation gives the artist/player a chance to put in some of their own artistry, (i) here, (ii) there and (iii) everywhere. However, in (iii) the tune will be lost, and listener/watcher will be wondering what's going on because the actual tune has been replaced by a 32-bar run of improvised melodic notes. A mix of notes from the melody intermingling with other notes could be better. For starters, the II-7, V jazz cadences appear often enough to make it worthwhile to learn off by heart some runs of notes based on the particular two chords constituting a cadence. So consider F-7/Bb7. The pianist may be playing SOLO or in a band, and it is easier if the chords are played (LH) at the same time as the RH plays the note run. Here is a run of notes for F-7 in solo or band.

NOTES	F	G	Ab	Bb	C	Bb	Ab	G	F
FINGERING	1	2	3	4	5	4	3	2	1

F-7

NOTES	Eb	D	C	D	Eb	D	C
FINGERING	3	2	1	2	3	2	1

Bb-7

Fig 6.1 (a) and (b)

These two chords can be played in one bar, so continuity must be preserved. This would mean 16 notes per bar. So try it out, practice it - solo timing less important. As improvisation takes its notes from scales, it should be noted that the two scales of a II V cadence are the same. The above 'runs' are the simplest of the simple 'runs', but you are also, at the same time playing two chords with the LH. This is just a start. Advance to more musical runs; bear in mind the tune.

6.1 Minor Chord Improvisation

Cadence Eb – 7/Ab7

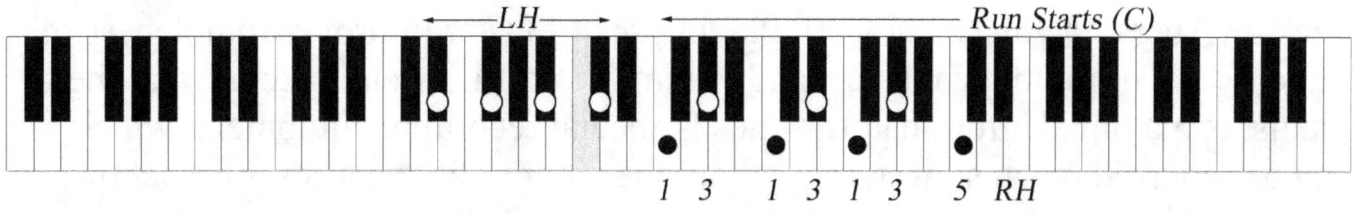

Fig 6.2(i)

CHORD Ab7 Dominant VII which follows from F of Fig 6.2(a)

Start at the top note C and follow from F to Fig 6.2(b) at G

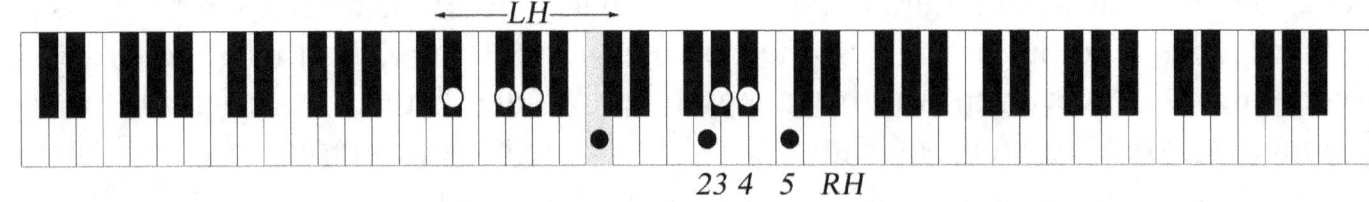

Fig 6.2(b)

LH chord can be played one octave lower. Already inverted to form a II V cadence wirh E*b*-7/

V7 cadence chord

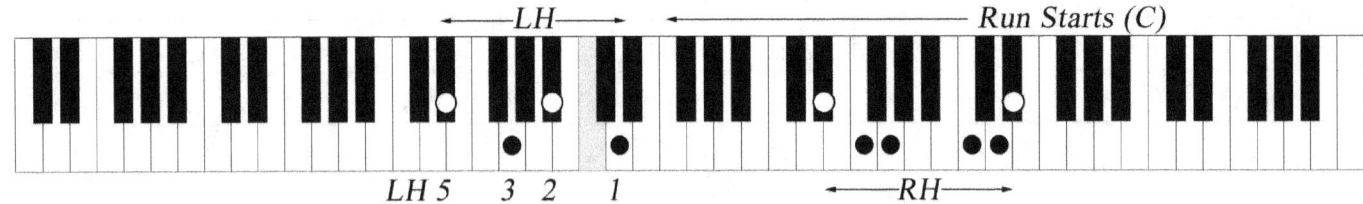

Fig 6.2(c) MAJOR

Chord E*b*Δ7

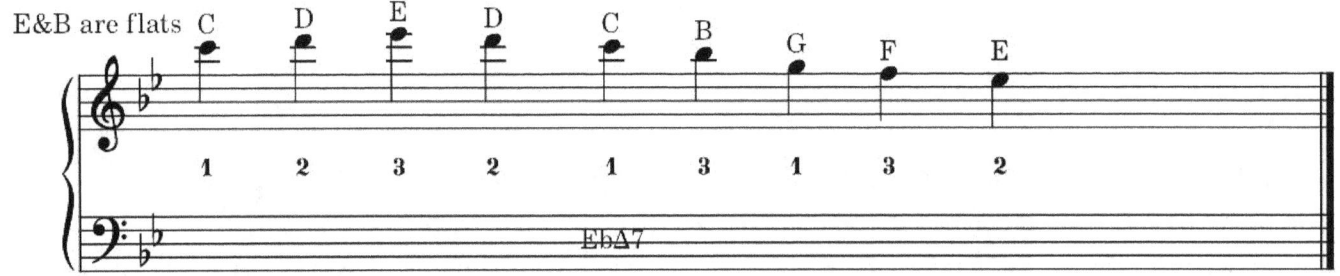

Fig 6.2(d)

THESE "RUNS ON NOTES" ARE EACH COMPLETED IN ONE BAR. This 'run' on E*b*Δ7 is not following Figs 6.2(i) & (ii) as the third chord of that cadence. They won't transpose very easily to other scales, but the players can write their own RUNS in other keys. These 'runs' can be speeded up or shortened, especially (i) and (ii) above to fit into one bar. They are, after all the two chords of a Il-7 V7 cadence. For further practice see references at the back on Abersold vols. 28 and 30. Playing scales faster improves nimbleness of fingers. You listen to the masters and you may not follow and take in what the pianist is playing. Unfortunately, it needs special recording equipment, which can be replayed much slower, to pick out the nature of the chords, or what the run of notes is. These musicians know just where they are, in a piece of music, they can leave gaps and yet not miss a beat. If you play in bands, your confidence will improve in time, and you will experiment with different chords. Jamey

Abersold's "*All Time Standards*" vol. 25 along with Steve Gilmore's "*Bass Lines*" (Transcribed from vol. 25) will enable you to listen and read the bass notes plucked. Each instrument can be heard separately (bass & drums, and piano and bass). This book is just a starter to playing higher level and may be used as springboard to better things. Read, listen, and play. There is always the possibility of inserting into a piece of music a "walking tenths exercise" (abbr. w10ths). Musically it is best to replace the second chord of a II-7 V7 cadence with the W10th. It is highly unlikely to be used in a band - there's no time, it would mess up the chord sequence. You will see in the following short article that it uses the top two notes of the second 4 note chord of the cadence, i.e. V7; these two notes are always separated by two tones. In the example below these two notes are C and E. To make an interval of a 10th, we move the top noter up by one octave. This 2-note chord is shown in FIG 6(iii) and forms the first chord of a sequence of 4. So below, you just follow the figures (iii), (iv), (v) and (vi). This sequence will take time to execute and follows musically because, as is well known it only needs the root and the third, and in the example shown this sequence follows G-7 (consult your circle of fifths).

6.2 Walking Tenths

(W10ths) are always used at the bass end of piano.

This topic is appropriately considered as a direct consequence of the II-7 V7 IΔ, cadence. The quickest way to describe the process of a II V cadence is to take G-7, C7 as the first two chords.

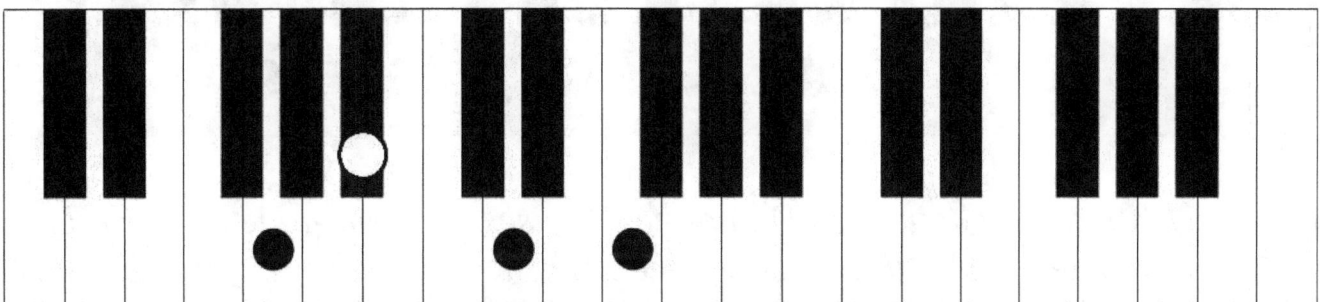

Fig 6.3 (i) G – 7

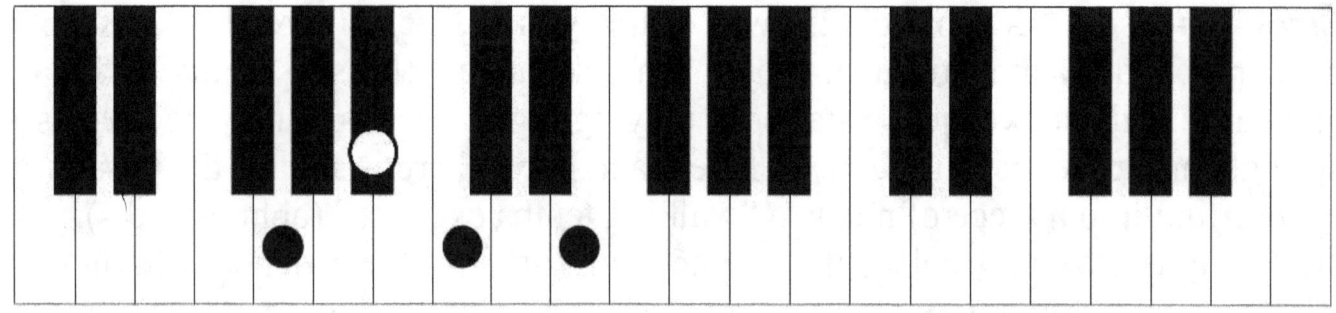

(ii) is C7 – top two notes C & E.

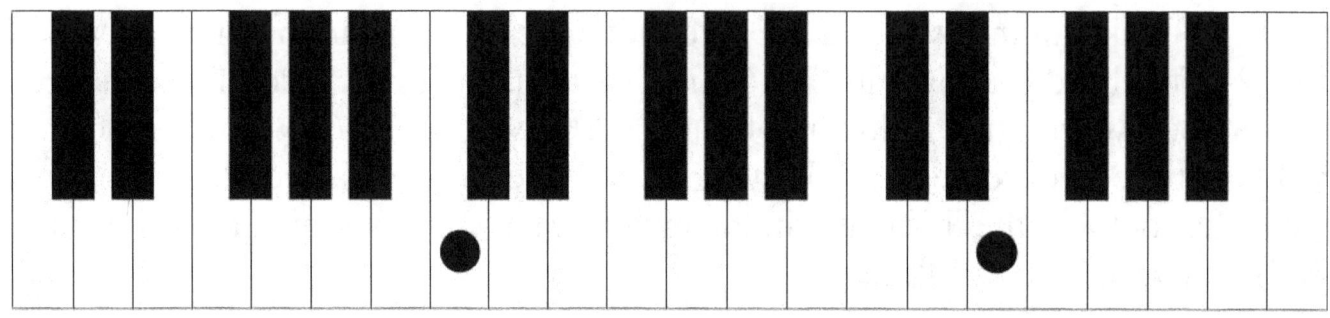

(iii) C & E are now played a 10th apart lower down the keyboard LH-C, RH-E

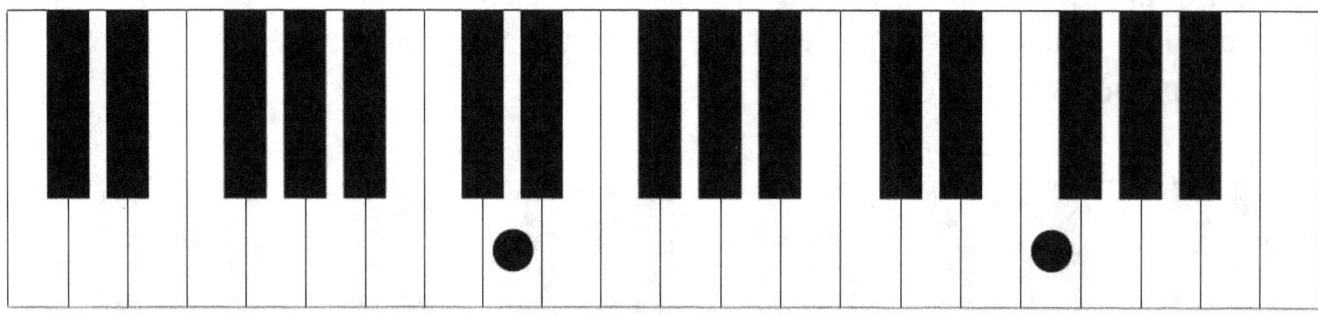

(iv) The LH rises one tone C to D and the RH rises one semi-tone (E to F). In the remaining three figures, the LH & RH notes all rise one semi-tone.

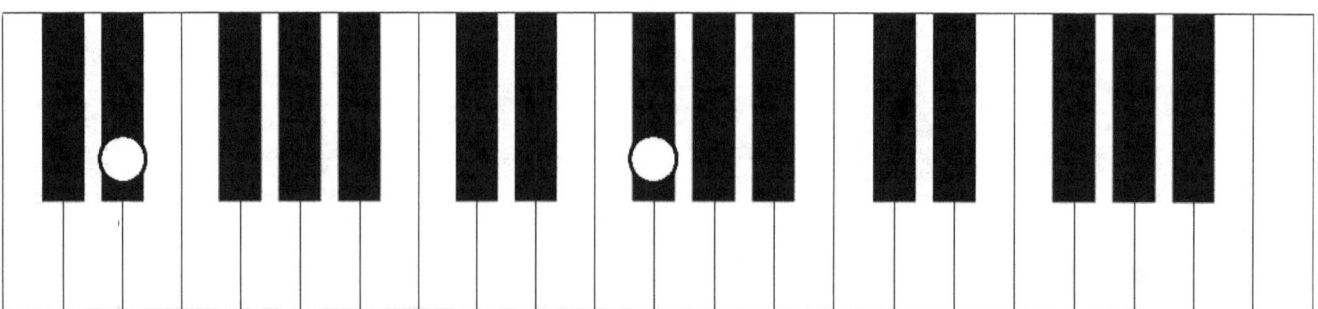

(v)

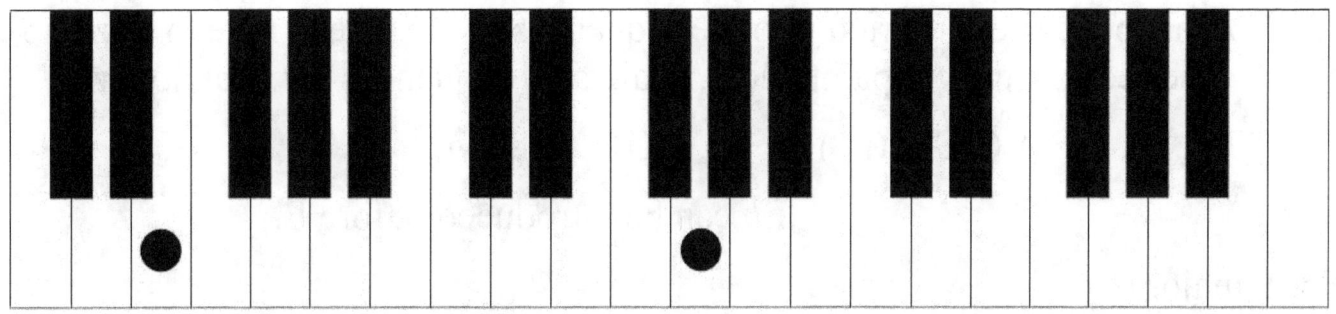

(vi)

Q4.1 Write down the first 2 notes of the W10th for

(i) F-7, Bb7

(ii) E-7, A7

6.3 Pentatonic chords/scale

As mentioned in the section on scales, it is appropriate to re-consider Pentatonic in 'improvisation'. John Dunstaple introduced in the early 1400's a powerful new chord combination[13]. It went chord I to IV to I to V to I. It could be summarised as I IV V.

These chords are:

```
    C   E   G (I) →      F   A   C (IV) →      G   B   D (V) Major Only
    ↑   ↑                    ↑                     ↑
  Major Minor              repeated              repeated
  third third          These are the intervals between notes
                  I              IV              V
```

The scales for each of these chords are CDE GAC, FGACDF and GABDEG (easily remembered scales, they're based on Gb, Ab, Bb, Db, Eb and Gb (black notes)). Previous improvisations used pictures of keyboard, but this time you're given 'dictated' piano notes instead.

  RH. C D E D E G A G A (up)   C C A G Eb/E C (down)

  Eb is introduced   Eb/E played almost together quickly.

Joining Eb to E 'jazzes up' the sequence, RH If these 15 notes are practised a few times, then they are maybe accompanied by the CEG I chord using LH. The player then shifts LH to chord IV (FAC) and with RH plays the fifteen notes starting FGAGACD... a fourth up. These notes are all transposed by a fourth.

Finally, LH plays chord V: GBD while the RH goes through the 'jazzed up'

---

13   Reference 6

sequence GABABDE DEGGED B♭/B G. These off the scale jazz notes E♭, and A♭, B♭, that have been inserted into the sequences of the fifteen note to 'jazz up', can be inserted as a truly separate note. A dictated sequences for C major are:

    C D D# E G A G C C (up)   A G E C (down)

                            E♭ can be introduced before E.

For F major (IV)

NOTES	F	G	A♭	A	C	D	C	F	F	D/D♭	C	A	F
FINGERING	1	2	3	1	2	3	2	5	5	1/3	2	1	3

The pentatonic education is not being dwelled upon anymore, as it is not often played in bands. All the above sequences of notes are the students' choice. You can 'jazz it up' in any way you want, including the length. Each time you play it will be an improvement. It is trial and error! Bill Evans, back in 1958, in music entitled: 'Peace Piece' showed how pentatonic scale could be improved on.

See ref.10

Chapter 7 - History of the Piano Keyboard

Development of the twelve note keyboard; and satisfactorily fitting in the intervals – semitones and tones.

This chapter is largely a diversion from playing piano notes and following instructions. You will learn about how piano music came into being. Starting with the octave (frequency f^0 rising to $2f^0$). Pythagorous living in the 6th century BC is attributed with the discovery of the constitution of the sound emanating from a Blacksmith's forgery. First the possibility of octaves, easily detectable by the human ear. Splitting the octave up a logical step by followers of Pythagorous, it was felt that a pitch halfway between the two sounds an octave apart, i.e. $(f^0 + 2f^0)/2 = 1½f^0$. That note would, in modern times be G, halfway up from middle C to the next C on the piano. No sophisticated treatment of sounding notes was available in the sixth century BC. The next stage of producing harmonically related numbers in a practical sense was by plucking a string, hearing the sound and varying the sound by adjusting the length between two fixed points, or by varying the tension (see fig 7.1a) ie, the weight w. Guitars (not in the centuries BC) have string tighteners, to tune. Sonometers are used in physics experiments; both tension and length can be varied by known amounts. Reeds are tubular and can give blown sound (used BC), the frequency depending on the length. You can blow into a milk bottle to produce sound, but the non-uniformity makes the pitch less predictable. FIG 7.1a is a picture of a string, under tension, with weight W, over the pulley wheel P. Like a guitar string and when plucked the string will vibrate as shown in (b). The string gives out a sound of frequency $f^0/2$, which is the fundamental frequency of course a guitar string is held at both ends i.e. no pulley P.

Striving for harmony throughout history

The harpsichord, akin to the grand piano, originated in the 15th century. The strings were horizontal and plucked; from this instrument the pianoforte was derived. The clavichord around the same time was in the form of a box, without legs, and the strings were plucked by means of quills. Compared to the modern pianoforte the early instruments produced a weak sound[14]. During the 17th and 18th centuries the harpsichord was developed in numbers and quality. The pianoforte also came in 1750. The twelve (semi) tone octave formed the basis of all stringed instruments, and theory of this is outlined in figures 7.1a to d. The attempt at finding the way to choose these semitones in the pianoforte for harmony is considered more deeply based on figures 7.2 and 7.3. 10.6 and 10.7 in the glossary.

---

[14] Note the suffix forte = strong

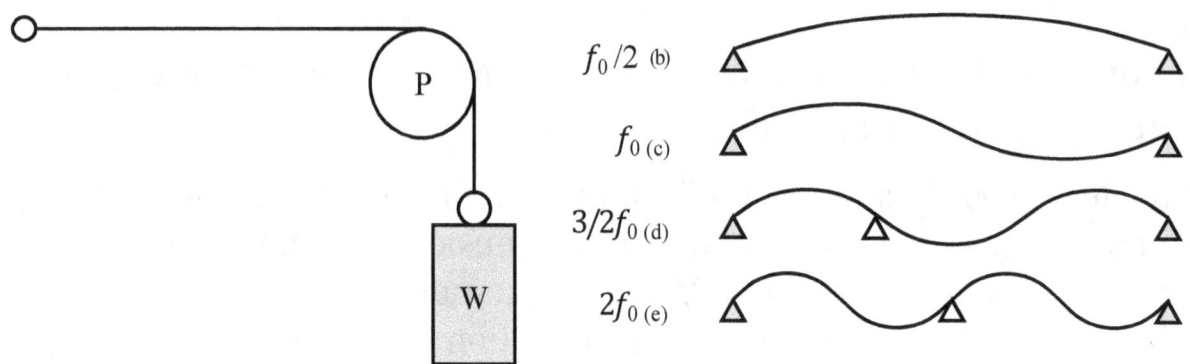

Fig 7.1 a-e

b) open string, freq $f^0/2$

c) an octave is produced on the plucked string (as in guitar, for instance) by fretting it halfway, is its mid-point.

It vibrates at twice its frequency; i.e. f^0 = fundamental. See also in the glossary under F (frequency)

d) By fretting a third of the way along the string, it vibrates $3/2 = 1½$ times its fundamental f^0

e) Frequency $3/2$ fundamental, $3/2 f^0$. This corresponds to the note at G above C. Demonstrated more easily by initiating from tuning fork. (Originally experements by Melde with one end of string $-2f^0$. – attached to tuning fork)

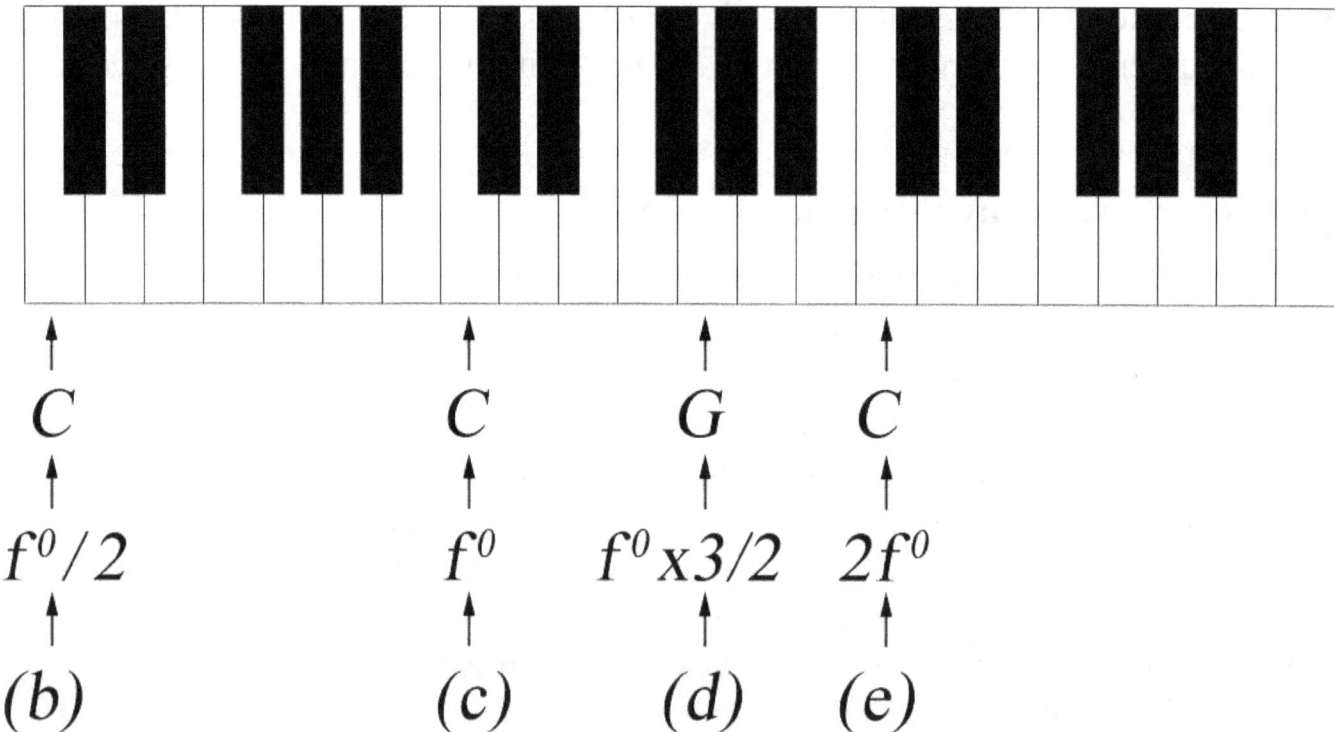

Fig 7.2

Harmony between piano notes/keys was considered to be possible provided the notes were related by simple numbers in ratio form, ex 2:1, 3:2, 4:3 and so on. Unfortunately, to arrange a series of successive notes (i.e. keys) as in Fig 7.2 had not developed successfully with Schonberg's twelve note proposals; but the progress toward dividing the octave into twelve equally spaced, man-made positions was slowly being developed. The first precise calculations of an equal temperament scale were made by V. Galilei. The so-called keyboard used lengths of plucked string, or bamboo pipes. Churches used organ pipes and Bach, being highly religious, drove development - the result, the Bach fugues, all fourteen of them. Bach was also actively developing the piano in Germany. The piano gained popularity in the 18th century. The invention of the piano, the mechanism: strings were hammered rather than being plucked (as in the harpsichord) had one great advantage, the harder you hit the keys, the louder the volume (forte). That was Cristofori's invention (Italian, during the 17th century – a mechanical invention for hammering. This invention could not be improved upon for a long time, it was so successful.

Let us go up in frequency from position O, first in fifth and then in fourths. These are shown in Figs 7.3 (a) & (b), and numbered 1,2,3 etc.

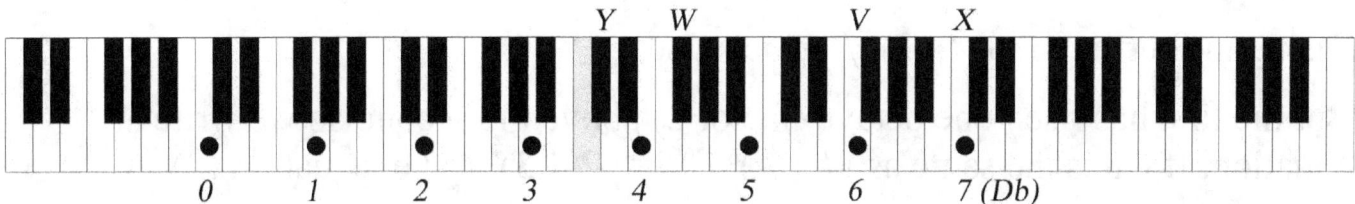

Fig 7.3(a) Rising in Fifths i.e. 3/2

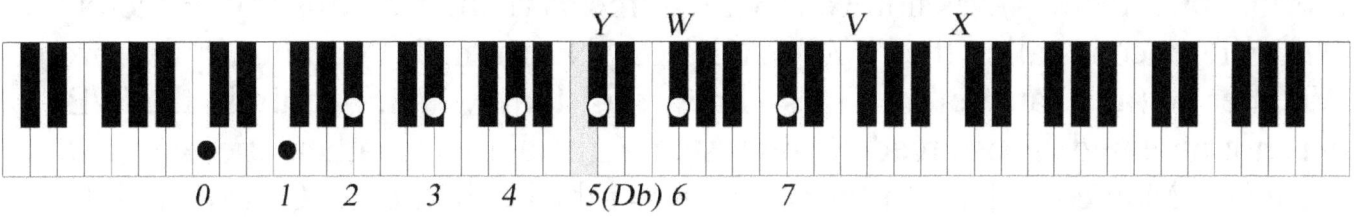

Fig 7.3(b) Rising in fourth i.e. 4/3. (See glossary under S. Semitones).

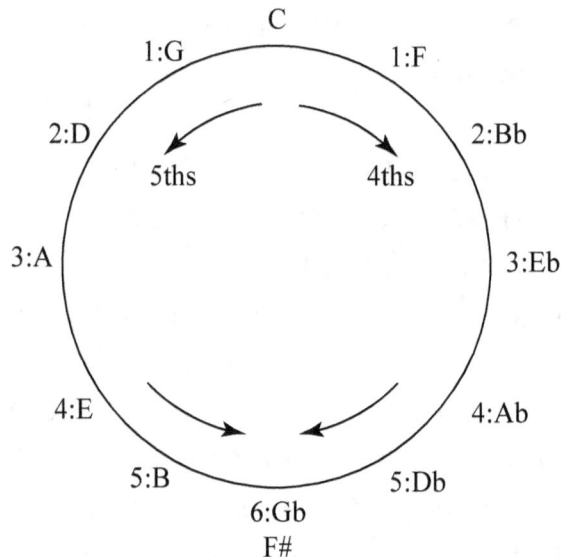

Fig 7.3(c)

In Figs 7.3(a) and 7.3(b) respectively, they both rise to a Gb or F#. After six movements (a) rises to one octave higher than (b) – V and W in the Figs. Going anticlockwise (Fig 7.3(c)) and Rising in fifths, F# $(3/2)^6 f^0$ - (1) (It rises $3/2$ x $3/2$ x 6 times). This is equation (1).

Rising in fourths, Gb is $(4/3)^6 f^0$ clockwise.

But the first has risen one octave (factor 2) above the second so we write an equation. If Gb is the same as F# $(3/2)^6 f^0$?=? $2(4/3)^6 f^0$ i.e. equation (2).

Arithmetic shows that these two expressions are not exactly equal, they have a ratio $3^{12}/2^{19} = 1.01364$ i.e. Gb is not quite the same as F#. So rising in so called fourths, by a factor 4/3 is not exactly the same as rising by fifths (by $3/2$ factor). The difference is called the "PYTHAGOREAN comma" (PG) after Pythagorous. Whether he (at a date before Christ) knew this, I know not, I doubt it, the K/B was not invented. Those readers interested in the above "mathematics applied to music" May consider a further point along the keyboard i.e. C# (See point X in fig 7.3(a)) and equate it to point Y (also C#) in fig 7.3(b). X and Y are two octaves apart. So we compare $(3/2)^7 f^0$ with $4(4/3)^5 f^0$. These have the same ratio as in the equation (2), which is 1.01364. Ideally the ratio should be 1.00, but in designing a keyboard on the basis of fourths, fifths and octaves there is an error of about 1% i.e. the difference between the LHS & RHS of equation 2 above.

In retrospect (many centuries ago) this was felt to be good harmony in progressing from C to F to G to upper C. But as seen in the present this progression, extended over four octaves doesn't quite work out (error is slightly over 1%). As stated this "small" error is possibly audible: - i.e. to musical instruments played out of tune by 1%. Pianos/keyboards are now designed to conform to "equal temperament". (see glossary under 'T'), whereby this error is made to vanish. It's basis is to make every successive note (.e. A to A#, B to

C, E to F etc. etc.) change its pitch (or frequency) by the same factor, chosen to make every octave (C to upper C, A# to upper A# etc.) double the pitch by exactly 2.000. Equal temperament came into design of the piano strings (i.e. their individual frequencies) in 1876 - organs and pianos. Up to that time the selection of individual frequencies of the strings (and lengths of the organ tubes/pipes) followed the earlier theory, it was called "Just Intonation". It will be seen that the Pythagorean system (octaves, fifths & fourths) can give a variety of answers to semitone values, and the so called "experts of the day" tuned the strings using different numbers. "Mean Tone Temperament" was used, and this resulted in certain keys being tolerable, and some unusable. The experts set the semitone in parts of the piano using $^{135}/_{128}$, or $^{25}/_{24}$, $^{16}/_{15}$. These ratios were obtained using only the three Pythagorean fractions, and working from different standpoints. You will see in the glossary -S (semitones) has the value 1.062.

Consonance and dissonance with "equal temperament" is about fitting notes together. Listeners would agree that some notes and some chords fit well together, whereas others fit less well. We feel that consonance is good, and dissonance is bad and unsettling. The desire for consonance drove 'musical designers' to look and search for scales of music that possessed harmony; hence the desire for notes related to one another by simple numbers in respect of tone. That idea has to some extent been demolished by the last few pages. This is not to say that notes separated by an interval of a third, fourth, or fifth are in discord. A piano chord formed from C and G is in harmony even though their frequencies are not exactly 3:2; if we take the extreme case of 2 notes separated by one semitone, they will sound discordant when played together. It is easily shown by simple theory that they beat together and produce a sound of distorted tone equal to the average of the two frequencies. The beat frequency is half of the difference of the two frequencies. For theory see in the glossary under BEATS. It is shown in the glossary that we have an undistorted chord (theoretically) made up of two frequencies if you like, but the sound really depends on the ear of the beholder. Jazz chords have advanced, flattened ninths, sharpened elevenths, see Fig 7.4. The list is endless in respect of dominant chords. The word dominant is used with 9th, 11th, 13th and of course 7th ($b7^{th}$) See reference 4.

The reader should play the following labelled chords. (a), (b), (c) are dominant chords. (Figs 7.4(a), (b) and (c)).

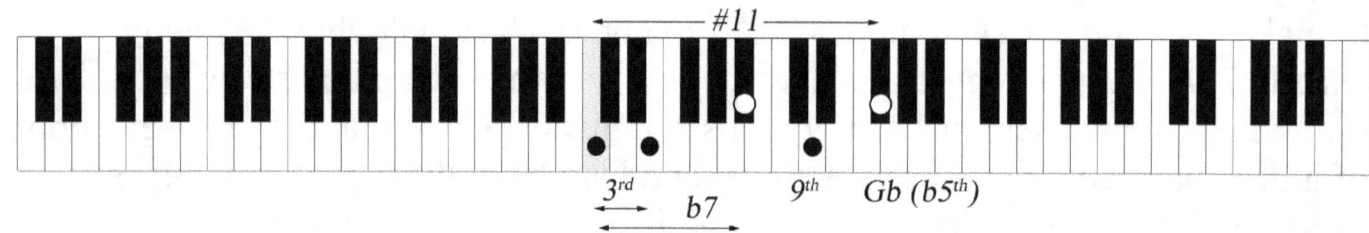

Fig 7.4(a) C9#11 with flattened 5th.

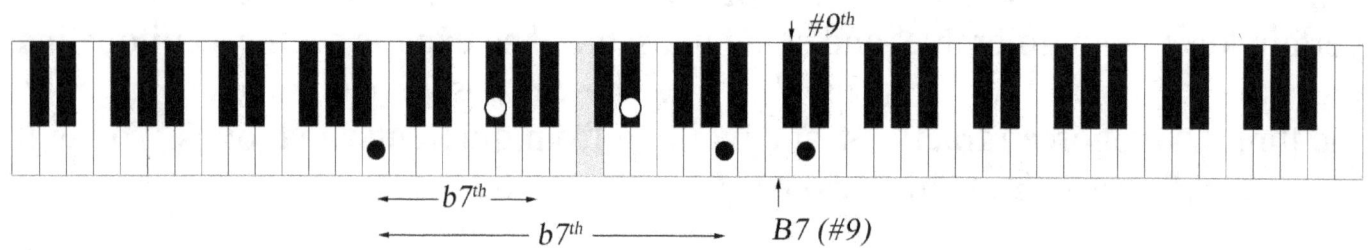

Fig 7.4(b) B7(#9)

All dominants have a minor 7th. Can be an octave up.

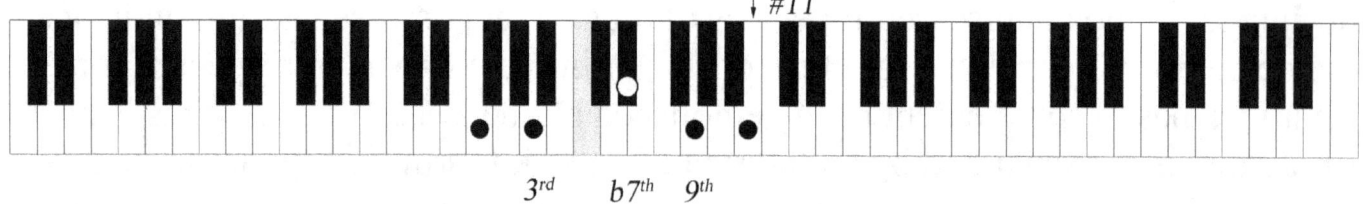

Fig 7.4(c) F9#11 with flattened 5th

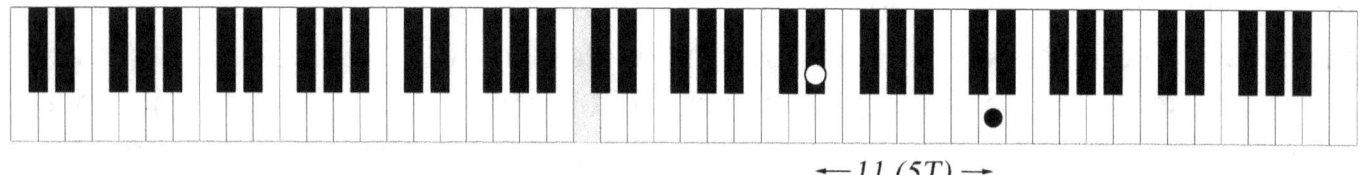

Fig 7.4(d) Hitchcock's chord 11 semitones

Just as beauty is the eye of the beholder, so consonance (or lack of it) is in the ear of the beholder and if you take your mind to the Bernard Herrman's score of Hitchcock's *"Psycho"*, you'll remember (and never forget!) the ear-piercing clash of two notes placed at a distance of 11 semitone. Figs (a), (b), (c)[15] and (d), show varying chords/dischords. You'll note that (a) and (c) are the same type of chord but different keys. Whether these two chords sound differently rather determine how well the piano is tuned (digital K/Bs should not go out of tune).

---

15   See Reference 4

Chapter 8 - Four sheets of music

8.1 Moment's Notice

Blue Trane J. Coltrane (SA) Music from blue note 534

(Note that in this chapter, rests have been omitted from the sheet music for simplicity)

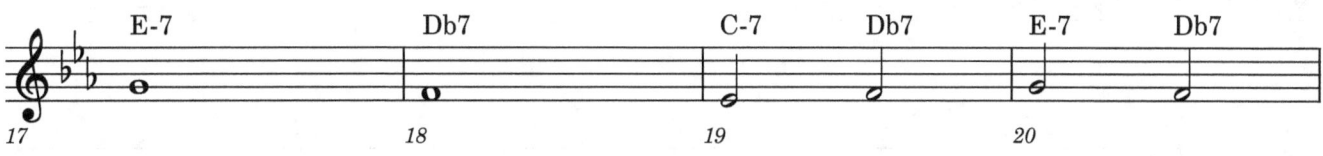

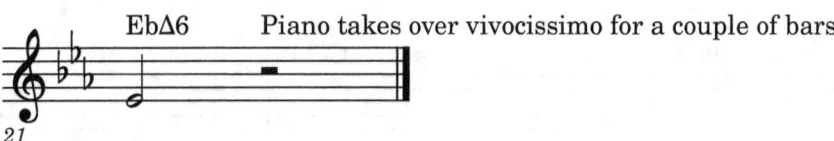

8.2 I'm Old Fashioned

Intro: Sax Accompanied By piano chords on CD

8.3 I'm Old Fashioned Solos

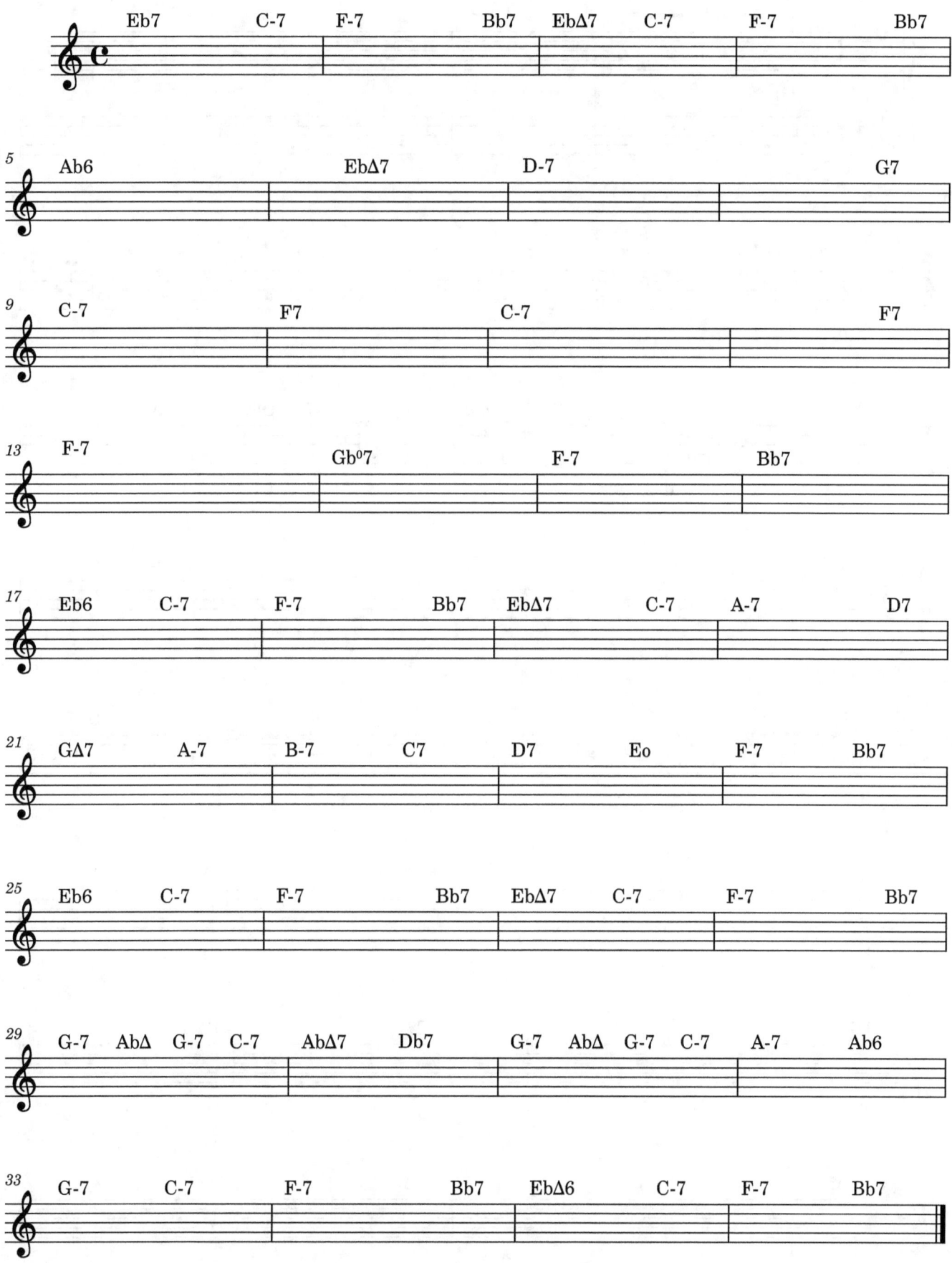

8.4 Lazy Bird

This piece is full of II, V and II, V, I jazz cadences, shown where they exist

Lazy Bird block Diagram

This block diagram ignores the first 5 bars, these are the intro.

A	A-7 D7	C-7 F7	F-7	Bb7	EbΔ7	A-7 D7	GΔ7Φ	Ab-7 Db7
A								GΔ7
B	B-7	E7	AΔ7	Bb-7 Eb7	A-7	D7	GΔ7	Ab-7 Db7
C	F7Φ	Eb7	A-7	D7	GΔ7	C7	FΔ7	Bb7
D	Eb7	AbΔ7	Db7					

Play to bar 24 (DC). Go to Head. At bar GΔ7Φ (8th column in table above), go to bar F7Φ (column 2 row4), play the last eleven bars.

This sheet of chords is to help students play the chords shown in the music, music uncluttered by melody lines. Improvisation is based on these chords as indicated in Chapter 6. There are 35 bars in this tune. Of course (in bands) these 35 bars need to be played in the time allotted. Metronome or CD.

8.5 Blue Trane, John Coltrane

Bb, Db, Eb, Gb, AB = FLATS

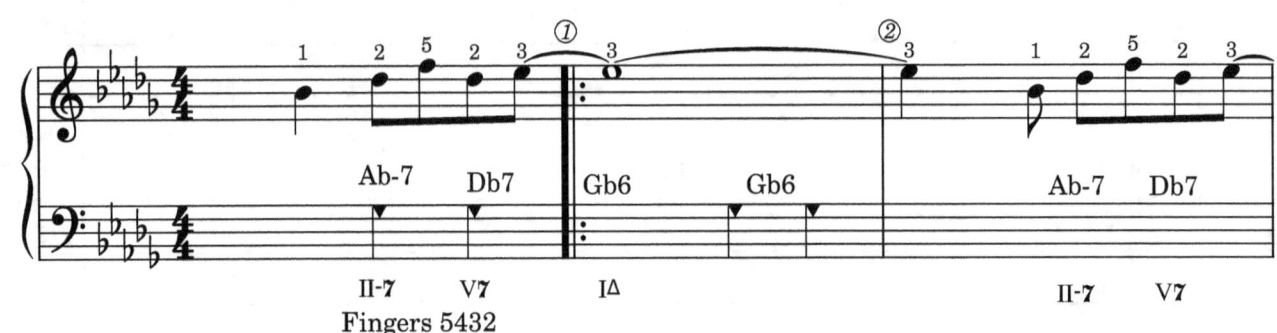

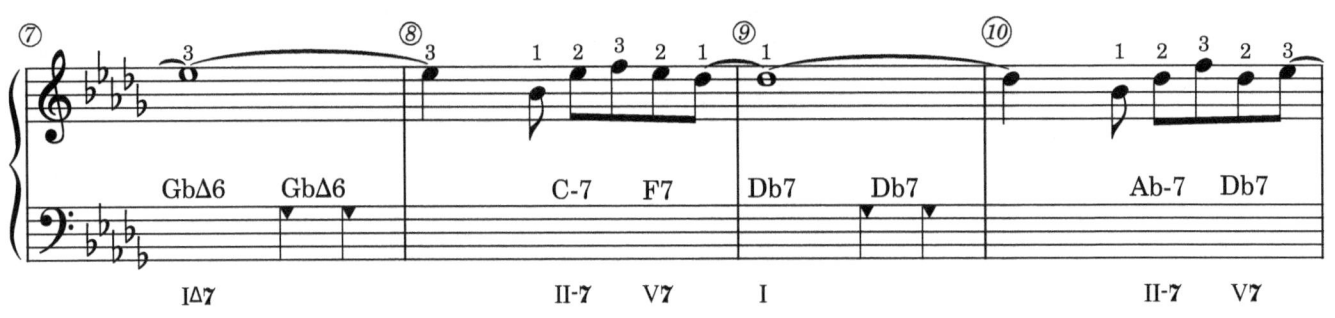

There is further detail in Chapter 5 re playing this piece.

Chapter 9 - Answers

Answers to Questions, with comprehensive hints.

Q2.1(i) A

Q2.1(ii) C

Q2.2 To work out the notes of a scale (minor in the examples below), the only aspect you have to remember is the constitution of the D. Dorian minor – the white notes of the piano. Sit at the piano, play the notes and write down the intervals (H or W) of this scale:

$$D \mid E \mid F \mid G \mid A \mid B \mid C$$

$$\uparrow \; \uparrow \; \uparrow \; \uparrow \; \uparrow \; \uparrow$$

FIRST ONE IS   W H W W W H   E to F = H   B to C = H

Below these arrows, use these intervals to write down successive notes for the scales of (i) A – 7 (ii) Eb – 7.

So there are: six intervals, seven notes.

A-7 =   A | B | C | D | E | F# | G

$$\uparrow \; \uparrow \; \uparrow \; \uparrow \; \uparrow \; \uparrow$$

W H W W W H

Six intervals

Eb-7 =   Eb | F | F# | G# | A# | C | G# |

$$\uparrow \; \uparrow \; \uparrow \; \uparrow \; \uparrow \; \uparrow$$

W H W W W H

Note that all minor scales have the same intervals:- WHWWWH - six of them.

The letters for Eb are each one semitone above their corresponding letter of D scale. I asked in this case for seven letters, because, of course the eighth letter of the scale is the same as the first letter (the root). It is so important that the number 7 appears in specifying most chords to distinguish them from mainly the numbers 6, 9, 13. It is very important to be able to reproduce most scales in order to improvise in tunes. You have to be prepared to play notes taken from the scales of chords in front of you, instantaneously. If the pianist is soloing in a band, these notes have to be played in the time specified by the music script. But when soloing on one's own, listeners won't notice timing errors.

Q2.3

(i) This is in Fig 2.6, but play and sing it, DOH, RAY,… LA, TE (seven)

(ii) $Bb\Delta 7$ = Bb C D Eb F G A (7)

(iii) $Db\Delta 7$ = Db Eb F F# G# Bb C (7)

Don't forget to sing DO RAY ME FA SO LA TE DO as you play the piano in these exercises.

(iii)   G7 = G A B C D E F   (major with flattened 7th)

   D7 = D E F# G A B C

Q3.3 $Gb7$ = Gb Ab Bb B Db Eb E.

If you play the Major scale in $Gb\Delta$. Then you flatten the major 7th (F) to E.

Q3.4

(i) $Ab\Delta 7$ = Ab C Eb G

(ii) $Gb7$ = Gb Bb Db E

(iii) EΦ = E G Bb D

(iv) Take the minor of C = C Eb G Bb.

The ½ dim. Chord has flattened fifth, G -> Gb.

Q3.5 Two handed chords. + is a sharpened 5th.

(i) F major with sharpened 5th (i) F F …, A C# E (G)

(ii) $Bb7+$ = Bb Bb … D F Ab (5th above Bb is F).

(iii) Dbo = Db Db … E G Bb (Db)

   1 2 3 4 or 5 Remember successive notes

   Separated by 3 semitones.

(iv) F13 ($b9$)

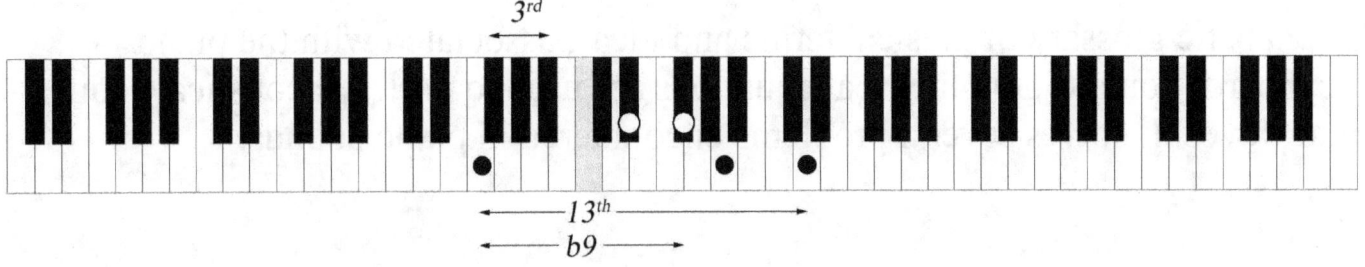

Q3.5

An interval of 13 from F reaches upper D. We consider 3rd & 7th as the most important notes in a chord, hence A and Eb. Flattened 9th is Gb.

Q4.1

(i) Bb and D.

(ii) A and C#. Each separated by two tones – one octave. Remember the rule on the rises that they are all semitones except the first LH one; this is one tone. In example 4.1(i). Bb rises to C, and D rises to Eb etc. From a musical point of view this W10th follows naturally from chord F-7.

Q4.1

F-7, Bb7

(i) Start Bb and D, C and Eb, C# and E etc. Each pair separated by a 10th.

(ii) E – 7, A7. Start A & C#, B & D etc. ALL pairs played at the bass end of piano and rising up.

Glossary

Alphabetic glossary of musical terms and ideas, associated with the piano/keyboard. Some trigonometrical equations are used to portray acoustical sounds and waves. It solves several problems encountered in piano sounds.

A

The note A above middle C is set at a pitch of 440 Hertz (cycles or vibrations per second). Middle C is around 256 Hertz. Arpeggio (like a harp).

Fig. 10.1

The wavy line indicates that the chord should be broken, or spread, usually upwards. The speed with which the notes are played is faster on a harp. It is loosely used describe a method of playing a chord on a piano, up or down, at a much slower rate. This procedure is a first step in improvisation, playing chords with the LH and "arpeggiating" them with the RH (broken chords).

LH CHORD ACCOMP   RH

Fig. 10.2

B

Beats

Beats occur when two sinusoidal waves are superimposed on one another. They interfere: So we take a simple trigonometric equation.

$\sin A + \sin B = 2\sin((A+B)/2) \cos((A-B)/2)$

Assuming equal amplitudes for two interfering waves. We take A & B as the two waves: - For example approximating to G# and G above middle C (mc). They represent the two piano notes. As these two notes are a semitone apart, then frequency of A is approx. 1.06 times B. See under S for semitone.

B approximates to 400Hz;

now A−B = B(A/B −1)

    = B(1.06−1)

    = 24Hz

A+B = B(A/B+1)

    = 824Hz

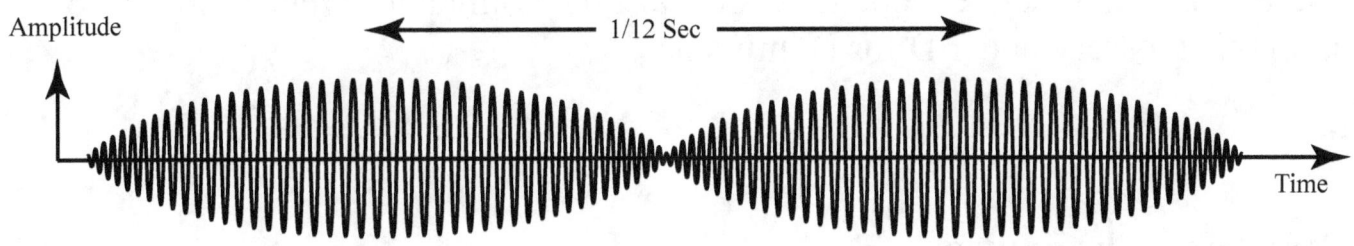

Fig. 10.3

SOUND	BEAT
Freq 412 Hz	Freq. 12Hz

The product of these two waveforms is an envelope of 12Hz, and a sound of 412Hz, i.e. (A+B)/2, which is halfway between the two notes. 12Hz is the frequency of the beat. As the separation in frequency goes up the result is that beating frequency rises and becomes inaudible, and we are left with two separate tones or if you like one note of frequency midway, (Midway between A & B is (A+B)/2 = frequency). When two notes G and G# are struck together, the listener hears the "whir whir whirring" or beating. They may hear the two individual sounds G and G#, or they may choose to hear just one sound which is halfway between G and G# (i.e A+B/2) which is 412Hz. The above treatment show how a simple trigonometric identity can give rise to interpreting the distorted (dissonance) sound that musicians are aware of.

Bass Clef

Played near the lower end of the piano. Five ledger lines marking spaces for notes A C E G. The base clef is not used in Jazz music in this book. It is replaced by chords.

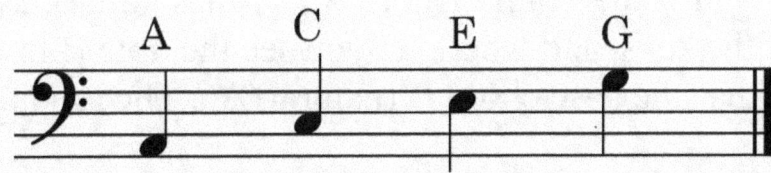

Fig. 10.4

Bright

This term is used only to describe a chord which engenders optimism in the listeners mood. It is associated with major chords. There is a sequence of chords that start with

(i) sadness (minor chord) and progress to

(iii) brightness.

There is an intermediate mood that is in Jazz the dominant seventh chord (look up in this glossary under D for Dominant).

C

Capo (Head) beginning

(Da Capo (DC) is under D).

Crochet ¼ note, ¼ bar.

Coda (Φ)

A sign at any point in music telling the player to go to some other point. (Called hot cross buns). Second Φ is placed where pianist continues.

Cadence

While this word has several meanings, only Jazz cadences are considered in this book. They are all II,V,I cadences, and are considered in chapter 4. The II V I is the most important for speedy chord change. It is abbreviation for II − 7 V7 IΔ7 i.e. Minor Dominant 7 Major.

Chord

Formed from two or more notes. These notes, when played single handed and in left hard form half the contribution to soloing. They must by necessity be within an interval (look up under I in glossary) of about an eighth or ninth chords and need to be memorized. NB. When reading jazz music with treble and chords, the notes forming the chord are completely determined by letter and number. The flats in this treble have no bearing on the notes in the chords. An example to use to make this point is in 'Blue Train'. Chord Ab − 7 has note B natural, yet in the treble Bb is one of the keys, and wherever you see the note B in the treble clef you play Bb. Bar 5 has the base chord B (natural) Δ6. The top note of this chord is Ab.

Chord symbols

Δ7 = major 7th, Dominant seventh is symbolised by the note letter & followed by the numerical 7, eg. G7, or C7. Minor symbolised by a line ex C – 7. The number 7 signifies that the 7th is played, & it is a flattened 7. It can be D7, G – 9, A13 etc. Diminished is symbolised by a zero, eg. Co or C dim. NB. A13 is called A Dominant 13. For solo players this chord will be played A7, as the LH is not big enough to stretch to a 13th. The major symbol Δ is left out, as in "I'm Old Fashioned" (Eb6)

Clef

Are the names of the notes on the staff. The treble clef staff is used purely for the melody notes played by one finger. Band piano players don't play the melody but 2 handed chords. The bass clef is not used for most jazz pieces; this includes real books and vocal new real books. So this book uses chords instead. These chords must be learned so that they can be played instantly – this applies for solo and band playing.

D

Da Capo

(D.C.) From (or to) the beginning (of a piece of music) or head.

Dal Segno

From the sign

Demi-semiquaver

1/32 of a bar

Fig 10.5

Dorian

Dorian is important as far as it specified minor scales in Jazz. It is most easily remembered of being the white notes in D minor, D up to D. There are two semitones in the sequence of notes (see chapter on scales). The Dorian has two semitones E to F, B to C. so the student can work out quickly any minor scale by transposition for each note.

Dominant

This refers to a cord, very frequently used. In simple terms we consider the major C scale C D E F G A B C and modify it by flattening (i.e. By lowering the pitch by a semitone) of the note B. Show the dominant chord in C becomes C E G B*b* = C7 CHORD. C to B is an interval of seven. Ignoring the fact that the B is flattened the number seven is preserved and defines most dominant seventh chords, F7, D7, G7 are symbolised by a letter followed by the number 7. It is in fact a minor seventh. See also in figs 7.4 (a) (b) and (c). These are also dominant chords: 9th, 11th, and 13th. These chords still contain flattened 7^{th}s, and are played solo, as 7th. Whereas two hands can cover higher intervals.

E

Enharmonic

Used when a note changes its name but not its pitch. Ex. F# becomes G*b*, B# becomes C. It may be recalled that there was a time when F# and G*b* did not have quite the same pitch. This was before equal temperament was invented.

F

Flat

Lowers a note one semitone in pitch. The symbol for flat is *b*.

F13 Dominant chord

Played as F7 when a solo player is using his left hand only for chords. Two handed chord players can span the 9th note and further (ex 13th) when needed. This latter situation applies to pianist in bands. The scale of F# and of G*b* are respectively:

F#	G#	B#	B	C#	D#	F	F#
G*b*	A*b*	B*b*	B	D*b*	E*b*	F	G*b*
Eight notes = 1 Octave							
DOH	RAY	ME	FA	SO	LA	TE	DOH

There are six sharps and six flats above. The CIRCLE OF FIFTHS makes the same statement. Are F# & G*b* in the same key? It is a matter of opinion as to whether the word **scale** covers 7 or 8 notes; does the DOH RAY ME… end on TE? I re-write the scale of F#:- F# G# A# B C# D# E# i.e. 7 notes and 6 sharps.

Equal temperament brings G♭ and F# to equality.

G

Guitar/Double bass

Guitar/Double bass players' plucked notes. How does the pianist respond to the bass player in a band? (Solo pianists – no worry). The figure below shows notes played by a professional bass player, vivo tempo = 200bpm. One bar therefore has a duration od 1.2 seconds.

Fig. 10.6

Definitely the root plus one of two from 3rd 5th, 7th are plucked. Readers of this book, who will have watched a good professional jazz band perform might think that the pianist has information passed by an earplug from an oracle who is speaking the bar numbers throughout the tune. On page 38 reference is made to good timing. See ref 8. Perhaps an easy way is using an electronic metronome. Set to say 32 bars, at an appropriate tempo. It shouldn't take many repetitions to achieve complete success, finishing on the 32nd bar, on time! Each individual will find his/her best way of responding to each chord, on time.

I

Interval

Used in music to describe the difference of pitch between two notes. Example C to G is an interval of a fifth because it (C D E F G) encompasses five notes C to G. The E and B are likewise an interval of a fifth. C to E is a third C to E♭ is a minor third, so we specify that C to E is a major third. When we get into sharps, we introduce another term, Diminished. So the interval between C to F# is a dimished fifth. Finally an octave is an eighth, C to C, F# to F#. (octagon – eight sided figure, octet – band of eight players).

Improper fraction

A fraction with numerator greater than the denominator. So a proper fraction is the opposite.

K

Key Signature

The Key is the note on which the music piece is built. The group of sharps or flats in a piece is called Key signature. For example, a piece of music written in the key of B*b* means that it must be in the scale of F major = F∆7. The sequence of notes forming this scale are F G A B*b* C D E F

(check by reciting DOH REY … DOH).

See circle of fifths for verification.

L

Logarithms

Logarithms are employed here to solve a problem $S^{12}=2$ i.e. Twelve semitones equal one octave. Theory: if $y=\sqrt[n]{x}$ i.e. the nth root of x, then $\log y = 1/n \log x$. So we look up log x, multiply by 1/n and take the antilog of that number. Calculators will have to be extra special to solv that problem. The answer is worked out as follows: Twelve semitones equals one octave. S^{12}, $S = \sqrt[12]{2}$. Look up (in Log., tables) log 2. So $S = 1/12 \log 2 = 0.3010/12$, $S=1.059$. So 1.059 x 1.059... 12 times = 2.

M

Minor Scales

Minor scales differ from major scales in respect of where the semi-tones are placed. In jazz, minor scales are DORIAN, look up, in the glossary, under D. See also "SYMBOLS" in the glossary. Major and minor are considered "bright" and "sad".

Minim

A half note or a half bar.

Middle C

So called because it's the middle of the piano. Abbreviated m c.

Major Scale

Major scale in C is a series of white notes C D E F G A B C = C∆. (1 Octave)

If you play this sequence on the piano you may, at the same time, sing DOH RAY

ME FAH SO LA TE DOH. This may help you play another major scale with flats or sharps. Take G major. Start playing at G and go up the scale, singing at the same time. Hopefully you'll find there id F# sharp in the octave G to G. For further info. see the chapter on scales. See the topic "SYMBOLS".

N

Natural

Restores a note to its original pitch. So for example B*b* becomes B natural.

O

Octave

The term given to a sound, double or half of a note of the same name. A-A, D-D, F#-F# (on a piano). 8ve placed above the treble stave means the music must be played one octave up.

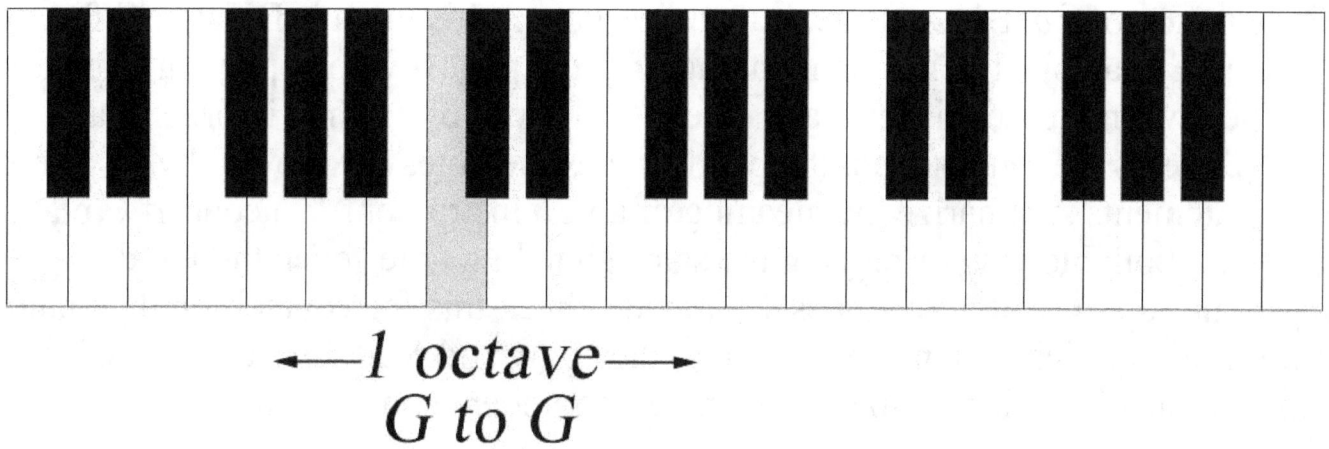

←—1 octave—→
G to G

Fig. 10.7

P

Piano keyboard

Shown above is one octave. Pictures of around 4 to 5 octaves are shown in several parts of the book. Middle C is shaded, it represents approximately the middle of a piano or keyboard. In the 'era' of piano invention, the word was "piano & forte" (Italian) – "Soft and strong" because unlike the Harpsichord (plucked) it could be played that way. This was abbreviated to pianoforte.

Q

Quadruple time

4/4 or C = Common time

Quaver

1/8 of a bar = ♪

Quaver rest = 𝄾

S

Sad

Describes tension in music (opposite of bright).

Saxophone (abbrev. Sax)

Explanation of E♭, B♭, A musical wind instrument. It's pitch is B flat or E flat. Take an E♭ sax playing in a band, along with the pianist who is playing in concert C. Then when the sax player reads note F# followed by B, then in order that a listener hears the same sound, the pianist reads the notes A followed by D. These two statements summarize the meaning of an E♭ instrument & a concert C piano. They are both blowing or playing the same sounding notes even though the music notes are written 1½ tones separated. Check this for yourself on the piano, note from both instruments even though they play and read different notes. This long explanation might help band members to understand the difference.

Scale

(latin "scala" a ladder) is an alphabetical succession of sounds, ascending or descending from a starting point.

	C	D	E	F	G	A	B	C
	DOH	RAY	ME	FAH	SOH	LAH	TE	DOH
Pythagorous	1	9/8	5/4	4/3	3/2	5/3	15/8	2
Equal temperament	1.000	1.122	1.260	1.335	1.498	1.682	1.886	2.000

Semibreve

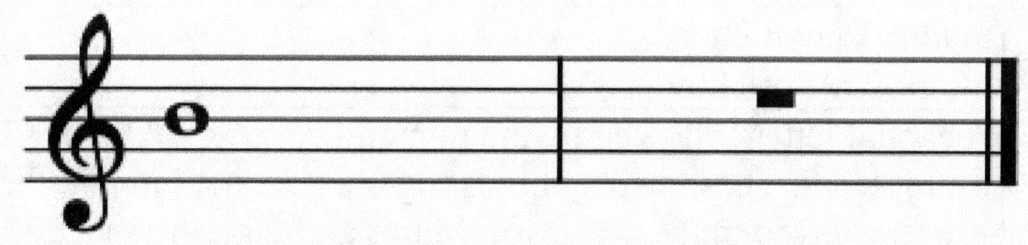

Fig. 10.8

Lasts one bar in time. It is a whole note.

Semitone

Exists between notes E and F, B and C. It is the smallest interval between two notes. To sharpen a note is to increase its value by a semitone. Historically harmony between notes was considered possible provided the notes were related by simple numbers 2:1, 3:2, 4:3 etc. The interval of fifth has been made to 3/2 (see CHAPTER 7). To represent therefore a semitone we calculate it from the fifth i.e. the ratio 3/2, in tones it is 3½ tones (ex C to G) or 7 semitones C D E F G. If the ratio of a semitone = S, thus $S^7 = 3/2$. Using logarithms (see under heading logarithm), compare with answer in section under heading L Logarithms. $S = 1/7 \log 1.5 = (0.176) 1/7 = 0.025$. S is found to be 1.062 and S^2 (a tone) is $1.125 = (1.062)^2$. A fourth interval (ex C to F) is 2½ tones or 5 semitones, or one tone less than $3/2 (= 1.500)$. $1.500/1.125 = 1.333$. This ratio (by good fortune) is 4/3; a simple ratio.

NOTE That one tone = 2 semitones = 1.062 x 1.062 = 1.125. It should be said that when we say "one tone less than 3/2", we are thinking factors; we do not subtract 1.125 from 1.500, we divide by 1.125.

Sharp

Symbolised by # represents all the black notes on a piano.

Staccato (Italian = detached)

Of an individual note(s) separated from its neighbours by a silence. Generally prescribed by means of a dot over the notes. Emphatic "staccatissimo" indicated by a wedge. Staccato is in "Blue Trane" in the second half of bars 1, 3, 5, etc. Piano and Drums sound in CD.

Staff

This consists of five parallel lines. Notes are placed on the lines, and between.

Symbols (in this book).

Δ	major scale or chord
--	minor scale or chord
A-G	A capital letter followed by the numeral seven = DOMINANT 7. For example F7. These two symbols together are stating that the music is to be played in the scale of F Major and with the seventh note flattened. This chord or scale is dealt with in more detail under the subject headings (i) Scales (ii) chords. Sign ',-', "CONTENTS" at the beginning of the book.
b	Flat. This symbol lowers the pitch of a note by one semitone.
#	Sharp. This symbol raises the pitch of a note by one semitone.
♮	Natural. This symbol restores the note to its original pitch. Semitone = the difference in pitch between B and C, also E and F in the major scale of C. i.e. CDEFGABC. All the other pitch differences between successive notes in the scale are tones or whole tones.
H	A half tone. W = whole tone. On Pythagorean scale, a tone was 9/8. On equal temperament scale was 1.122. Semitone = 1.06.

Sync

Perhaps this word is slang, it has been used once. Out of sync – out of time.

T

Temperament (History).

Galileo's father (initial V) proposed in 1581 that a semitone should correspond to factor 18/17. Twelve such steps should give the 1.9855 for an octave; this would result in fourth & fifth not being exactly correct. So finally it was accepted that the equal temperament scale giving $5^{12} = 2$ i.e. $5 = {}^{12}\sqrt{2}$ for a semitone (called a twelfth root of two). This was accepted for future development of the Piano. It gives the fourth a factor 1.3348, and the fifth – 1.4983. These two figures are Slightly better than using the figure 18/17 for a semitone, by B. Galileo. His Fourth & Fifths were 4/3 & 3/2 approximately.

Tie or Bind

A crochet plus a quaver. A note is sounded till the end of the quaver

Timing

Lengths of various notes

Note	Shape	Rest	Name
Semibreve	𝐨	▬	Whole Note
Minim	𝅗𝅥	▬	Half Note
Crotchet	♩	𝄽	Quarter Note
Quaver	♪	𝄾	Eight Note
Semiquaver	𝅘𝅥𝅯	𝄿	Sixteenth Note

One Tone = Two semitones = 1.122 (equal temperament).

Treble

The Great Stave consists of eleven lines (see Fig. 10.9) The treble clef (TC) circles round the G line.

Fig. 10.9

Tritone Substitution

The following three chords form a typical ending to a piece of music D – 7, D♭ 7, CΔ7; they are played in succession, the middle chord is dominant 7th. They can be played in any key, by transposition calculation.

W

Wholetone

A wholetone = two half tones. It is symbolised by the letter W. It represents the difference in pitch between certain notes in the C major scale:

C major = C∆ = C D E F G A B C (octave = 5W + 2H)

       ↑ ↑ ↑ ↑ ↑ ↑ ↑
       W W H W W W H

The difference in pitch between C and D, F and G, etc. are wholetones. In a scale of 1 octaves, if its major or minor scale is played there are 5 W and 2 H's. W = 2 semitones. H = 1 semitone, so in one octave: 12 semitones. In the wholetone scale, there are 6W's in one octave.

Wholetone Scale. Thelorius Monk invented this scale; he became more famous after he died. He showed Coltrane how to play several notes at a time on the saxophone! "Working with Monk brought me close to a musical architect of the highest order" said Coltrane.

Woodwind Instruments

Includes recorder, Clarinette and (surprisingly) saxophone even though this instrument is not made of 'wood', it's metal; it has a single reed. In jazz the brass instruments include trumpet & trombone, bugle & French horn, and other lip-reed instruments.

X

Xylophone

(pronounced z, Zylophone): Percussion, set up like a piano & made of metal. Strictly speaking from personal experience this popular Jazz is called a vibraphone (shortened vibes). It is struck with mallets. The famous musician by the name of Milt Jackson, played vibes with two mallets. He was famous in the MJQ, up to the fifties (1950). The new vibes players use four mallets. they do appear in the Proms at the Albert Hall, the musicians also play a wooden version called marimba. Evelyn Glenie should be mentioned, because this lady has played in concertos. She was (and still is) an expert in all percussion (this includes untuned percussion i.e. drums etc.). I've had the privilege of attending one of her courses (at Woburn). The amazing thing is - she's deaf. The vibrations (i.e. sound) are picked up by some other parts of the anatomy!

References

1. CD to purchase: *John Coltrane - The Ultimate Blue Train*, Blue Note CDP 7243 8 53428 0 6
   (Contains the four tunes included in this book)
   https://www.discogs.com/John-Coltrane-The-Ultimate-Blue-Train/release/16302213
   Amazon. **https://amzn.to/3nc4OVf**

2. Abersold, J, On Improvisation, two volumes 30 (Rhythm section) 26 Scale syllabus PO BOX 1244, New Albany, IN 47151 – 1244, USA.

3. Ball, Philip, *The Music Instinct*, (The Bodley Head, 2010). Could be a copy in your local library.

4. Regarding chords, there are several books on this subject – "Jazz chords". Any good local musical shop in your locality.

5. Cork, Conrad, *Harmony by LEGO*, (Tadley Ewing Publications, 1985) Could be out of print.

6. Grigson, *The Jazz Chord Book*. This book is not to be confused with Ref 4.

7. *The Real Book.* 472 pages of Jazz:- Bossas, waltzes, med, fast, slow melodies. A must for playing in bands. (Hal Leonard, PO BOX 13819)

8. Gilmore, Steve, Abersold, J, 17 *All Time Standards*. Bass lines. Transcribed from *17 All Time Standards*, the latter from vol.25.

9. (i) Mehegan, John, J*azz Improvisation*: *Tonal and Rhythmic Principles,* (Watson – Guptill Publications N.Y. Amsco Publications New York/London/Sydney). Prefaced by late Leonard Bernstein

   (ii) Garcia, Russell, *The professional Arranger*, Composer, Book 1 (Criterion Music Corporation).

10. Evans, Bill, *Peace Piece* (CD no: 274247981, 1958). Uses pentatonic notes with improvised RH cascades.

11. *Circle of Fifths.* History dating from 17th century was this sequence of chords. Many classical composers have used it. *Story of Music* (Chatto & Windus, 2013).

Acknowledgements

I wish to thank Rosemary Howel (BA LOND) for help in diagrams and wording in this book. Also I am grateful to David Brownlow, DIP MUS, for valuable discussions regarding content.

Thanks also to Andy Severn of Oxford eBooks for his technical assistance in laying out this book for print.

Dedication

My interest in Jazz Piano was aroused on entering a weekly course (Saturday AM) throughout about 30 weeks given by Conrad Cork (Author of Harmony by LEGO) and past lecturer in Jazz at De Montfort University, Music School.

Contacting the Author

The author may be contacted by email for further discussionand help with the topics raised in this book: tcedric483@gmail.com

If there are many requests by readers, then I can organise a gropup meeting at a suitable venue,

www.ingramcontent.com/pod-product-compliance
Lightning Source LLC
Chambersburg PA
CBHW050718090526
44588CB00014B/2334